KINGDOMish

Boundaries, Barriers, and Beliefs that Hinder Kingdom Living Integration

Kim Parks

MBKLA Press

An imprint of Master Builders Kingdom Leadership

Kingdomish

Copyright © 2025 by Kim Parks

All rights reserved. No part of this book may be reproduced, distributed, or transmitted in any form or by any means, including photocopying, recording, or other electronic or mechanical methods, without the prior written permission of the publisher, except in the case of brief quotations embodied in critical reviews and certain other noncommercial uses permitted by copyright law.

Published by MBKLA Press

An imprint of Master Builders Kingdom Leadership Academy

Oakland Park, Florida, United States

ISBN: 979-8-9999510-0-7

Printed in the United States of America

DEDICATION

To those who refuse to settle for partial faith.

This work is for every Kingdom citizen called to wholeness, formation, and full alignment with the King.

Contents

CHAPTER 1 1
CHAPTER 2 11
CHAPTER 3 20
CHAPTER 4 30
CHAPTER 5 39
CHAPTER 6 48
CHAPTER 7 59
CHAPTER 8 69
CHAPTER 9 78
CHAPTER 10 87
CHAPTER 11 101
CHAPTER 12 111
CHAPTER 13 120
CHAPTER 14 128
CHAPTER 15 136
CHAPTER 16 143
EPILOGUE 151
RECOMMENDED READING 153
ABOUT THE KINGDOM FORMATION SERIES 155
APPENDICES 156
READER'S CHARGE 167
ABOUT THE AUTHORS 169
NOTES / INDEX 172

FOREWORD

Kingdom-ish sounds comfortable—edgy even. The title reveals our tendency to reduce faith to a commodity: a means to feel important, to add another book to our shelves, or to post about what we've read instead of how we've been transformed. Let's make one thing abundantly clear: this book—and this series—was not written to indulge that impulse. It was written to dismantle it. Together we confront the illusions that keep us comfortable, and together we offer a path into the hard but beautiful work of transformation.

What we as the Christian community have done is dangerous: we have mastered performative Christianity without yielding to the government (Kingdom) of Christ. We name it plainly, we trace how we got here, and—most importantly—we show the way out. The path we lay down is not trendy or filtered. It is Romans 12:2 in real time: a mind renewal that refuses cultural formation, heart surgery that collapses our self-made altars, and practices that produce obedience even when emotions don't.

If you want inspiration without transformation, go ahead and close this book. Scroll TikTok and keep drifting. But if you are weary of drifting through your spiritual experience and ready for substance, keep reading.

Kingdom-ish

The architecture of the journey is deliberate:

Kingdom-ish but Kingdom-filled. Not more information—reorientation. This opening move exposes the boundaries, barriers, and beliefs that keep us tamed, then calls for the only renovation that works: surrender that rewires how we think, choose, and live.

Identity before strategy. We anchor authority in adoption. You are not hustling for a seat at the table; you are already seated with Christ. His work is complete, and grace abounds! We must believe we are who He says we are, not who we think we are. That's not motivational talk—it's the only foundation sturdy enough to carry holiness, courage, and mission into Monday morning. Psalm 146:3 gives us a simple truism that keeps our trust and identity oriented properly to the King.

Barriers named, not romanticized. Legalism, relativism, dogma, orphan-minded striving and begging, conformity—none of it is brushed aside. We show you where those walls came from, how they masquerade as safety, and how to tear them down with repentance, humility, Spirit-dependence, and accountable community.

Culture engaged, not escaped. Salt that preserves. Light that exposes. Justice that isn't borrowed from politics but born from God's character. You'll receive practices that translate belief into public faith—at home, at work, and within social spaces.

Legacy and finish line. This isn't a solo sprint. We think in generations and end with the horizon: all things new. That future isn't an escape hatch; it's fuel for faithfulness now.

What we respect most is the transparency. The data about drift in the Western church isn't weaponized; it's a wake-up call. The language studies aren't academic displays; they're tools that return Scripture to its native force. And the practices—Scripture meditation, fasting from noise, confession and healing, rule-of-life rhythms, intergenerational mentoring—are simple enough to begin this week and sharp enough to keep cutting years from now. This alone is a game-changer.

Expect to be challenged in three specific ways:

Your mindset. This book will force you to decide whether you truly trust and live by the Spirit—not only in how you feel on Sunday, but in how you think at midnight and express yourself on Tuesday.

Your allegiances. You cannot carry the Kingdom and your pet idols together. Something has to die. We are merciless (and right) about that.

Your outputs. If your faith can't be audited in your calendar, budget, language, and relationships, it's still "ish." The chapters on ethics, justice, and leadership read like an integrity stress test—because that's exactly what they are.

All is not doom and gloom. You'll also find hope here—the stubborn kind. Not cheap optimism, but the confidence that the King always will and always has finished what He starts: in a person, a family, a church, a city, or a nation. The call will require more of you, but it is not complicated. Seek first the Kingdom and His righteousness. Refuse the drift. Practice the disciplines. Build people and systems that will outlast you. Keep your eyes on the horizon and your hands on the plow.

We are grateful this book exists. It was written with the kind of conviction you cannot fake, a conviction we share and can vouch for. We refuse to settle for partial faith, and we invite you to bring that same refusal to these pages—no excuses, no performance, no spectatorship. If you do, Kingdom-ish will not be your story much longer.

Let's get to the real thing. May our conviction become yours, and may you follow this light to your next spiritual horizon—where obedience replaces performance and the Kingdom becomes your way of life.

Ezra Pryor; Founder of One Pryority, Co-Author of Kingdom-ish

PROLOGUE

Kingdom-ish invites readers on a profound journey into the heart of Kingdom living—an experiential path to discovering identity in Christ, deepening communion with the Father, and embracing our divine calling as citizens of God's Kingdom. This journey transcends intellectual understanding; it is a vibrant, Spirit-led progression toward maturity in Christ, self-transformation, and readiness for the return of our King.

Along the way, you will encounter critical milestones:

Kingdom Mindset (Kingdom-ish) — Readers will experience a reorientation of thought, vision, and identity, breaking free from boundaries, barriers, and limiting beliefs. This book awakens them from "Kingdom-ish" living into the fullness of Kingdom life.

King's Kings — Readers will be equipped to embrace their calling to rulership under Christ. They will learn how to steward authority, govern with integrity, and live as delegated kings under the King of Kings.

Kingdom Proper — Readers will enter the stage of Kingdom maturity, experiencing deeper obedience, power, and alignment. This book prepares them to walk as the mature Bride of Christ, living daily in expectancy of His return and the consummation of His reign.

Each milestone builds upon the last, guiding you through introspection, growth, and transformation. Kingdom-ish is not merely a book but a call to step boldly into the fullness of your Kingdom destiny, empowered by the Holy Spirit and the Word of God

CHAPTER 1

The Gospel of the Kingdom: Truth Without Distraction

Introduction: The Message That Cannot Be Compromised

When Jesus first stepped into public ministry, His opening words set the stage for the entirety of His mission:

> *"From that time Jesus began to preach, saying, 'Repent, for the kingdom of heaven is at hand.'"*
>
> *Matthew 4:17*

This declaration was not casual, nor was it meant to be reduced to a slogan. The gospel of the Kingdom is not a subset of the Christian faith; it is the whole of God's redemptive story made manifest in Christ. The word gospel comes from the Greek euangelion (εὐαγγέλιον), meaning "good news" or "glad tidings." The good news was not simply that sins could be forgiven but that God's reign (basileia – βασιλεία, "rule" or "kingdom") had broken into the world through His Son. The Kingdom is not a theory or philosophy; it is God's government advancing in human life and history.

To reduce the gospel to inspiration or routine is to fall short of God's intent. Truth must be proclaimed without distraction. Studying

Scripture without revelation may make us learned but not transformed. The Pharisees were masters of memorization and performance, but when the Living Word stood before them, they could not perceive Him. Why? Because revelation only comes to surrendered hearts.

Jesus confirmed this in His exchange with Peter:

> *"And Jesus answered him, 'Blessed are you, Simon Bar-Jonah! For flesh and blood has not revealed this to you, but my Father who is in heaven.'"*
>
> *Matthew 16:17*

This is the heart of the Kingdom gospel: truth revealed by God, not constructed by human preference.

God's Original Intent and the Fracture of Sin

In the beginning, God's purpose was unmistakable. Humanity was created to bear His image, to reflect His nature, and to steward His creation in partnership with Him.

> *"So God created mankind in his own image, in the image of God he created them; male and female he created them."*
>
> *Genesis 1:27*

The Hebrew word for image, tselem (צֶלֶם), implies representation — humanity was created to manifest God's rule on the earth visibly. The word for likeness, demuth (דְּמוּת), suggests resemblance — we were to live in alignment with His character. This was God's original intent: image-bearers who carried His presence, walked in His authority, and lived in His likeness.

Yet, sin fractured this design. In Genesis 3, deception entered the garden. The serpent's lies produced doubt, disobedience, and separation. Presence was disrupted, identity was lost, and worship was corrupted.

> *"And the great dragon was thrown down, that ancient serpent, who is called the devil and Satan, the deceiver of the whole world—he was thrown down to the earth, and his angels were thrown down with him."*
>
> *Revelation 12:9*

Paul affirms this same truth:

> *"In their case the god of this world has blinded the minds of the unbelievers, to keep them from seeing the light of the gospel of the glory of Christ, who is the image of God."*
>
> *2 Corinthians 4:4*

Deception is more than ignorance; it is blindness of the mind. The Greek word typhloō (τυφλόω), "to blind," is used here to show the spiritual incapacity of humanity apart from revelation. Sin created not just separation but delusion — a deliberate clinging to falsehood in defiance of God's truth.

Delusion: The Condition of Fallen Humanity

Delusion is not simply confusion or lack of clarity. It is the intentional persistence in falsehood even when truth has been revealed. Paul captures this in Romans:

> *"For although they knew God, they did not honor him as God or give thanks to him, but they became futile in their thinking, and their foolish hearts were darkened. Claiming to be wise, they became fools, and exchanged the glory of the immortal God for images resembling mortal man and birds and animals and creeping things."*
>
> *Romans 1:21–23*

The Greek word for futile, mataioō (ματαιόω), conveys emptiness, worthlessness, and deception. Humanity knew God but chose to believe lies instead.

This is why Jesus rebuked the Pharisees:

> *"You are of your father the devil, and your will is to do your father's desires. He was a murderer from the beginning, and does not stand in the truth, because there is no truth in him. When he lies, he speaks out of his own character, for he is a liar and the father of lies."*
>
> *John 8:44*

The Pharisees were zealous for religion but devoid of revelation. Their delusion bound them to performance without presence. This is the problem with religion absent revelation: it makes us busy, passionate, and ritualistic, but not transformed.

Jesus: The Reset of God's Plan

Into this fractured and delusional state of humanity, God enacted His reset. Paul writes:

> *"But when the fullness of time had come, God sent forth his Son, born of woman, born under the law, to redeem those who were under the law, so that we might receive adoption as sons."*
>
> *Galatians 4:4–5*

Jesus is the perfect human, the true image-bearer, the one who fulfills God's original intent. He is the eschatos Adam (ἔσχατος Ἀδάμ), the "last Adam," who succeeds where the first Adam failed (1 Corinthians 15:45). Through His death, burial, resurrection, ascension, and enthronement, He resets creation's trajectory.

> *"Therefore, if anyone is in Christ, he is a new creation. The old has passed away; behold, the new has come."*
>
> *2 Corinthians 5:17*

The phrase "new creation" translates kainē ktisis (καινὴ κτίσις). The word kainos does not mean "new" in the sense of time (neos) but "new in quality" — something unprecedented, fresh, and transformed. Through Christ, we are not patched-up versions of ourselves; we are fundamentally made new.

Isaiah prophesied this reality:

> *"For behold, I create new heavens and a new earth, and the former things shall not be remembered or come into mind."*
>
> *Isaiah 65:17*

Here, the Hebrew chadash (חָדָשׁ) is used, meaning renewed, restored, made fresh. God's reset through Christ is not regression to the old but progression into the new.

Truth Without Distraction

The gospel of the Kingdom is the truth that must be proclaimed without distraction. Paul warned the Galatians:

> *"But now that you have come to know God, or rather to be known by God, how can you turn back again to the weak and worthless elementary principles of the world, whose slaves you want to be once more?"*
>
> *Galatians 4:9*

The danger is always the temptation to turn back — to lesser knowledge, outdated constructs, or religious systems that appeal to human pride. Legalism, denominational divisions, cultural idolatries, and political entanglements all distract from the simplicity of the Kingdom. Freedom is not found in preference; it is found only in truth.

Jesus declared:

> "So Jesus said to the Jews who had believed him, 'If you abide in my word, you are truly my disciples, and you will know the truth, and the truth will set you free.'"
>
> John 8:31–32

Truth liberates. Preference enslaves. Tradition binds. Revelation frees. This is why our mandate is "All Kingdom, All the Time." Any other message leaves people in bondage.

Looking Forward, Not Backward

The Kingdom gospel is forward-looking. It is about embracing God's newness rather than longing for old constructs. Paul captures this posture:

> "But one thing I do: forgetting what lies behind and straining forward to what lies ahead, I press on toward the goal for the prize of the upward call of God in Christ Jesus."
>
> Philippians 3:13–14

Looking backward keeps us bound to lesser revelation. Jesus warned of this reality:

> *"Jesus said to him, 'No one who puts his hand to the plow and looks back is fit for the kingdom of God.'"*
>
> *Luke 9:62*

God's Kingdom is always advancing. Revelation 21:5 assures us of the trajectory:

> *"And he who was seated on the throne said, 'Behold, I am making all things new.' Also he said, 'Write this down, for these words are trustworthy and true.'"*
>
> *Revelation 21:5*

To look back is to cling to the brokenness of sin's residue. To look forward is to embrace God's reset and transformation.

The Gospel and Transformation

Transformation is the evidence of Kingdom truth. Without transformation, the gospel has not been fully received. Paul exhorts:

> *"I appeal to you, therefore, brothers, by the mercies of God, to present your bodies as a living sacrifice, holy and acceptable to God, which is your spiritual worship. Do not be conformed to this world, but be transformed by the renewal of your mind, that by testing you may discern what is the will of God, what is good and acceptable and perfect."*
>
> *Romans 12:1–2*

The Greek word metamorphoō (μεταμορφόω), "to transform," is used here. It implies a radical change of form, not surface adjustment.

Transformation affects presence (we become temples of the Spirit), identity (we are adopted as sons and daughters), and worship (we yield ourselves fully to God).

Transformation restores what was fractured in Eden. It heals identity confusion, overcomes cultural delusion, and empowers true worship in Spirit and truth.

Conclusion: Truth That Transforms

The gospel of the Kingdom is not a fragment of Christianity; it is the fullness of God's intent for creation. It confronts delusion, restores identity, and ushers us into transformation. It calls us to truth without distraction, freedom without preference, and revelation without compromise.

Through Christ, God has reset humanity's trajectory. He has made us new creations. He has turned us from the darkness of delusion to the light of revelation. And He has called us not to look back, but to strain forward into His newness, until the day when all things are made new.

Glossary of Key Terms

- Basileia (βασιλεία): Kingdom, reign, rule.
- Euangelion (εὐαγγέλιον): Gospel, good news.
- Malkuth (מַלְכוּת): Hebrew word for kingdom, reign.
- Tselem (צֶלֶם): Image, representation.
- Demuth (דְּמוּת): Likeness, resemblance.
- Typhloō (τυφλόω): To blind, render incapable of sight.
- Mataioō (ματαιόω): Futile, empty, deceptive.
- Eschatos Adam (ἔσχατος Ἀδάμ): The last Adam, title for Christ.
- Kainos (καινός): New in quality, transformed.
- Chadash (חָדָשׁ): New, renewed, restored.
- Metamorphoō (μεταμορφόω): To transform, complete change of form.
- Huiothesia (υἱοθεσία): Adoption, placement as sons and daughters.
- Paristēmi (παρίστημι): To present, yield fully.

CHAPTER 2

Revelation vs. Delusion: The Battle for Truth

Introduction: Why Revelation Matters

Every generation faces a critical choice: will we live by the revelation of God or by the delusions of human imagination? Revelation is not intellectual discovery or philosophical speculation. It is the divine unveiling of truth to hearts surrendered to God. Without revelation, the gospel of the Kingdom is reduced to information—something studied, debated, or even admired but never transformative. With revelation, however, truth becomes living, active, and penetrating.

The Hebrew word galah (גָּלָה) means "to uncover, reveal, make naked." It is the lifting of a veil so that something hidden is now seen. The Greek equivalent apokalypsis (ἀποκάλυψις) means "an uncovering, disclosure." This is the word Paul uses when he speaks of the gospel he received:

> *"For I would have you know, brothers, that the gospel that was preached by me is not man's gospel. For I did not receive it from any man, nor was I taught it, but I received it through a revelation of Jesus Christ.*

> *Galatians 1:11–12*

Delusion, by contrast, is the willful rejection of revelation in favor of falsehood. It is not mere ignorance; it is the persistence in lies even when confronted with undeniable evidence. The Greek word planē (πλάνη) means "error, deception, wandering." Paul describes the state of fallen humanity in Romans:

> *"For although they knew God, they did not honor him as God or give thanks to him, but they became futile in their thinking, and their foolish hearts were darkened. Claiming to be wise, they became fools, and exchanged the glory of the immortal God for images resembling mortal man and birds and animals and creeping things."*

> *Romans 1:21–23*

The battle, then, is between revelation that frees and delusion that enslaves. This chapter will explore the necessity of revelation, the reality of delusion, and the way God calls us into discernment for transformation.

The Nature of Revelation

Revelation is not invention. We do not create truth; we receive it. Truth originates in God and is made known to humanity through His Spirit.

Jesus told His disciples:

> *"When the Spirit of truth comes, he will guide you into all the truth, for he will not speak on his own authority, but whatever he hears he will speak, and he will declare to you the things that are to come."*
>
> *John 16:13*

The Greek word for guide, hodēgeō (ὁδηγέω), means "to lead along a road." Revelation is a journey led by the Spirit, where truth is disclosed progressively as we submit. It is not a one-time event but an ongoing unveiling.

Moses longed for God's presence in the wilderness. When offered the help of an angel, he refused and pleaded:

> *"And he said to him, 'If your presence will not go with me, do not bring us up from here. For how shall it be known that I have found favor in your sight, I and your people? Is it not in your going with us, so that we are distinct, I and your people, from every other people on the face of the earth?'"*
>
> *Exodus 33:15–16*

Moses understood that revelation is not merely about words but about presence. God's presence reveals who He is and who we are. Without revelation, we are left with information but no transformation. With revelation, our identity is clarified, and our path becomes distinct.

Delusion: The Counterfeit of Revelation

Delusion mimics revelation by offering what seems like wisdom but is rooted in falsehood. Paul warns the Colossians:

> *"See to it that no one takes you captive by philosophy and empty deceit, according to human tradition, according to the elemental spirits of the world, and not according to Christ."*
>
> *Colossians 2:8*

The word "captive" here translates sylagōgeō (συλαγωγέω), meaning "to carry off as spoil, to kidnap." Delusion imprisons by capturing minds through ideology, tradition, and culture. It blinds people to the revelation of Christ and leaves them worshiping preferences instead of truth.

Jesus rebuked the Pharisees for their delusion:

> *"This people honors me with their lips, but their heart is far from me; in vain do they worship me, teaching as doctrines the commandments of men."*
>
> *Matthew 15:8–9*

The Pharisees mistook their traditions for revelation. Their worship was vain (mataios – μάταιος, "empty, useless") because it lacked Spirit-given truth. Delusion thrives in environments where form is elevated over substance, eloquence over discernment, and zeal over revelation.

Biblical Case Studies of Delusion and Revelation

From Genesis to Revelation, Scripture records the tension between revelation and delusion.

Adam and Eve (Genesis 3): They knew God's command yet chose the serpent's deception. Delusion distorted identity and disrupted presence.

Israel in the wilderness (Exodus 32): Having received revelation at Sinai, they quickly turned to the golden calf. Delusion masqueraded as worship but was idolatry.

Saul and David (1 Samuel 15–16): Saul was deluded by his own preference and disobedience; David, though flawed, sought revelation through worship and repentance.

The Pharisees (John 8): They rejected the revelation of Jesus standing before them, proving that religious zeal without revelation is bondage.

Paul (Acts 9): Once deluded in persecuting the Church, Paul was transformed by the revelation of Christ on the Damascus road.

These examples show that delusion is not limited to the ignorant or irreligious; it often ensnares the religious and the zealous. Revelation is the Spirit's gift to those who surrender.

The Cost of Delusion in Our Day

Delusion today takes many forms: denominational pride, political idolatry, cultural relativism, legalism, materialism, and the worship of personality. Churches divide over race, politics, and ideology rather than uniting under Christ. People celebrate leaders for eloquence rather than truth. Many pursue emotional highs in worship but lack discernment.

Paul describes the peril:

> *"For the time is coming when people will not endure sound teaching, but having itching ears they will accumulate for themselves teachers to suit their own passions, and will turn away from listening to the truth and wander off into myths."*
>
> *2 Timothy 4:3–4*

The Greek word for "itching" (knēthō – κνήθω) conveys craving novelty or pleasure. This is the culture of delusion: craving words that soothe rather than truth that transforms. The danger is not ignorance but willful rejection of truth.

The Necessity of Discernment

Discernment is the Spirit-empowered ability to distinguish revelation from delusion. John writes:

> *"Beloved, do not believe every spirit, but test the spirits to see whether they are from God, for many false prophets have gone out into the world."*
>
> *1 John 4:1*

The word dokimazō (δοκιμάζω), "to test," was used of testing metals for authenticity. Discernment requires careful evaluation of teaching, culture, and experience in light of God's Word. Without discernment, delusion flourishes.

Discernment is not rooted in emotion. Emotions may mislead, but revelation anchors us in truth. True revelation may not excite us; it may silence us, convict us, or even make us tremble. Isaiah experienced this when he encountered God:

> *"And I said: Woe is me! For I am lost; for I am a man of unclean lips, and I dwell in the midst of a people of unclean lips; for my eyes have seen the King, the Lord of hosts!"*
>
> *Isaiah 6:5*

Revelation produces awe, humility, and transformation, not mere excitement.

Transformation Through Revelation

Revelation is not an end in itself; it leads to transformation. Paul writes:

> *"And we all, with unveiled face, beholding the glory of the Lord, are being transformed into the same image from one degree of glory to another. For this comes from the Lord who is the Spirit."*
>
> *2 Corinthians 3:18*

The Greek word anakalyptō (ἀνακαλύπτω), "to unveil," describes the lifting of the veil through Christ. As we behold Him, we are transformed (metamorphoō – μεταμορφόω). Revelation thus bridges presence, identity, and worship. It restores what was fractured in Eden.

Conclusion: Choosing Revelation Over Delusion

The battle between revelation and delusion is not theoretical; it is lived daily. Revelation calls us to surrender, presence, worship, and identity in Christ. Delusion tempts us to cling to tradition, ideology, and preference. Revelation frees; delusion enslaves

Paul's challenge is ours:

"Have I then become your enemy by telling you the truth?"

Galatians 4:16

Truth is often unwelcome, but it is the only path to transformation. Our calling is to deliver truth without distraction, revelation without compromise, and the gospel of the Kingdom without dilution. Only then will delusion lose its grip and transformation take root.

Glossary of Key Terms

- Galah (גָּלָה): Hebrew, to uncover, reveal.
- Apokalypsis (ἀποκάλυψις): Greek, revelation, unveiling.
- Planē (πλάνη): Error, deception, delusion.
- Typhloō (τυφλόω): To blind, render incapable of seeing.
- Mataios (μάταιος): Empty, vain, useless.
- Sylagōgeō (συλαγωγέω): To capture, carry away as spoil.
- Hodēgeō (ὁδηγέω): To guide, lead along a way.
- Dokimazō (δοκιμάζω): To test, examine for authenticity.
- Anakalyptō (ἀνακαλύπτω): To unveil, uncover.
- Metamorphoō (μεταμορφόω): To transform, change of form.

CHAPTER 3

Transformation and the New Creation Reality

Introduction: More Than Change, A New Creation

The Kingdom of God is not about mere improvement; it is about transformation. God is not interested in polishing the old or patching the broken. His intent is to make all things new. The gospel of the Kingdom declares that through Jesus Christ, humanity is not offered self-improvement but rebirth. We are not offered advice on how to be better versions of ourselves, but an invitation into a new creation reality.

Paul captures this with absolute clarity:

> *"Therefore, if anyone is in Christ, he is a new creation. The old has passed away; behold, the new has come."*
>
> *2 Corinthians 5:17*

The Greek phrase kainē ktisis (καινὴ κτίσις) means "a new creation," not "renovated" but qualitatively new. The word kainos signifies new in essence and kind, while ktisis means creation, the act of making.

Together, they describe the radical work of God in the believer—something unprecedented, distinct from what came before.

Transformation is not cosmetic; it is ontological. It touches the very essence of who we are.

To understand transformation, we must trace God's redemptive timeline. From the fall of Adam to the cross of Christ, the narrative of Scripture is the story of God's resets: moments when He realigns humanity with His original intent. Transformation is always God's initiative, and it always calls us out of delusion into truth.

The First Reset: Adam to Noah

God created humanity in His image for relationship, dominion, and worship. Yet sin disrupted identity and corrupted creation. Genesis describes the spread of wickedness:

> *"The Lord saw that the wickedness of man was great in the earth, and that every intention of the thoughts of his heart was only evil continually. And the Lord regretted that he had made man on the earth, and it grieved him to his heart."*
>
> *Genesis 6:5–6*

The Hebrew word for intention, yetser (יֵצֶר), conveys the shaping or framing of thought. Humanity's inner framework had been bent toward evil. God's response was judgment by flood, but within that judgment was a reset through Noah. Yet even Noah's generation did not bring lasting transformation. Humanity's corruption persisted because the inner nature was still fractured.

The Covenant Reset: Abraham

God called Abram out of idolatry to become Abraham, the father of faith. This covenant established Israel as God's chosen people, set apart to display His holiness.

> *"And I will establish my covenant between me and you and your offspring after you throughout their generations for an everlasting covenant, to be God to you and to your offspring after you."*
>
> *Genesis 17:7*

The Hebrew word for covenant, berith (בְּרִית), means an oath-bound relationship. This covenant was a divine reset, yet Abraham's descendants repeatedly chose delusion over revelation. Though the law later given through Moses defined holiness, it could not transform the heart.

The Kingship Reset: David

God established David as king, a man after His own heart. Through David, God promised a throne that would endure forever.

> "Your house and your kingdom shall be made sure forever before me. Your throne shall be established forever."
>
> 2 Samuel 7:16

The Hebrew word olam (עוֹלָם) means eternal, perpetual. The Davidic covenant pointed forward to Christ, but even David's lineage fell into corruption. Israel's kings succumbed to idolatry, proving again that external systems could not accomplish inner transformation.

The Final Reset: Christ

All previous resets pointed toward the ultimate reset in Jesus Christ. He is the fulfillment of God's promises, the climax of God's redemptive plan, and the inaugurator of a new creation.

> "But when the fullness of time had come, God sent forth his Son, born of woman, born under the law, to redeem those who were under the law, so that we might receive adoption as sons."
>
> Galatians 4:4–5

The Greek word huiothesia (υἱοθεσία) means adoption, the placing of one as a son with full rights. Transformation through Christ is not simply about forgiveness; it is about adoption, identity restored, and inheritance secured.

Through His death, burial, resurrection, ascension, and enthronement, Christ enacted the final reset. His resurrection inaugurated the age of new creation, His ascension enthroned Him as King, and His Spirit empowers transformation in those who believe.

Transformation vs. Conformity

Paul contrasts transformation with conformity:

> *"Do not be conformed to this world, but be transformed by the renewal of your mind, that by testing you may discern what is the will of God, what is good and acceptable and perfect."*
>
> *Romans 12:2*

The Greek word for conform, syschēmatizō (συσχηματίζω), means to be pressed into a pattern, to assume an outward form not reflective of inner change. By contrast, metamorphoō (μεταμορφόω), "to transform," indicates an inner change that radiates outward. Conformity imitates culture; transformation reflects Christ.

The renewal of the mind (anakainōsis – ἀνακαίνωσις) is not about acquiring new facts but being fundamentally reoriented by the Spirit. Revelation renews thinking, reshaping how we perceive God, ourselves, and the world.

Identity Restored

Transformation is inseparable from identity. Humanity lost its identity in Adam, but in Christ, identity is restored. Paul writes:

> *"For you did not receive the spirit of slavery to fall back into fear, but you have received the Spirit of adoption as sons, by whom we cry, 'Abba! Father!' The Spirit himself bears witness with our spirit that we are children of God."*
>
> Romans 8:15–16

Fear enslaves, but adoption liberates. The Spirit testifies to our identity as God's children. The Greek word Abba (Ἀββᾶ) is an intimate Aramaic term meaning "father" or "daddy." Transformation restores intimacy, replacing fear with sonship.

Worship as Transformation

Transformation is expressed in worship. Worship is not a weekly event but a lifestyle of yielding ourselves to God. Paul calls believers to present their bodies as living sacrifices:

> *"I appeal to you therefore, brothers, by the mercies of God, to present your bodies as a living sacrifice, holy and acceptable to God, which is your spiritual worship."*
>
> Romans 12:1

The Greek word paristēmi (παρίστημι) means to present, to place at one's disposal. Worship is the daily act of surrender, the yielding of every aspect of life to God's will. This surrender forms character, reshapes priorities, and fuels transformation.

Presence as Transformation

Transformation requires the presence of God. Like Moses, we must refuse to move without Him. God's presence distinguishes His people:

> *"And he said, 'My presence will go with you, and I will give you rest."*
>
> *Exodus 33:14*

The Hebrew word for presence, panim (פָּנִים), literally means "face." Transformation comes by beholding God's face, by living continually in His presence. This is why Paul describes believers as those who behold the glory of the Lord with unveiled faces and are transformed into His likeness (2 Corinthians 3:18).

The Danger of Delayed Transformation

Many remain trapped in cycles of conformity because they resist transformation. Paul asked the Galatians:

> *"You were running well. Who hindered you from obeying the truth?"*
>
> *Galatians 5:7*

Delusion hinders obedience. When we cling to old constructs, outdated knowledge, or lesser revelation, we prevent transformation. God's call is always forward. Transformation is the evidence that we are not looking back but pressing toward His newness.

Living as New Creations

To live as a new creation is to embody Kingdom reality. It means carrying God's presence into every sphere of life, living with a renewed mind, and walking in holiness. Peter exhorts:

> *"But as he who called you is holy, you also be holy in all your conduct, since it is written, 'You shall be holy, for I am holy.'"*
>
> *1 Peter 1:15–16*

The Greek word hagios (ἅγιος) means set apart, consecrated. Transformation sets us apart not by isolation but by holiness. Holiness is not withdrawal but distinction. It is life lived in alignment with God's character.

The Consummation of Transformation

Transformation now is a foretaste of what will be fully realized in the future. John's vision declares:

> *"Then I saw a new heaven and a new earth, for the first heaven and the first earth had passed away, and the sea was no more. And I saw the holy city, new Jerusalem, coming down out of heaven from God, prepared as a bride adorned for her husband. And I heard a loud voice from the throne saying, 'Behold, the dwelling place of God is with man. He will dwell with them, and they will be his people, and God himself will be with them as their God. He will wipe away every tear from their eyes, and death shall be no more, neither shall there be mourning, nor crying, nor pain anymore, for the former things have passed away.'"*
>
> *Revelation 21:1–4*

Here again, the word kainos appears. God's work of transformation will culminate in cosmic renewal. The Kingdom will be fully realized, and humanity will dwell in God's presence forever.

Conclusion: Transformation as the Kingdom Mandate

The gospel of the Kingdom is transformation. Anything less is incomplete. God's original intent was fractured by sin, but through Christ, He has enacted the final reset. Transformation restores identity, reestablishes worship, and renews presence. It is not optional; it is the essence of Kingdom life.

To live as Kingdom citizens is to live as new creations. It is to embody God's future in the present, to demonstrate His holiness in a fractured world, and to walk in revelation rather than delusion. Transformation is the mark of those who have embraced the gospel of the Kingdom—truth without distraction, revelation without compromise, and newness without regression.

Glossary of Key Terms

- Kainē Ktisis (καινὴ κτίσις): New creation.
- Kainos (καινός): New in quality, transformed.
- Neos (νέος): New in time, recent.
- Yetser (יֵצֶר): Formation, intention, framework of thought.
- Berith (בְּרִית): Covenant, oath-bound relationship.
- Olam (עוֹלָם): Eternal, perpetual.
- Huiothesia (υἱοθεσία): Adoption, placement as sons.
- Syschēmatizō (συσχηματίζω): To conform, assume outward form.
- Metamorphoō (μεταμορφόω): To transform, change of form.
- Anakainōsis (ἀνακαίνωσις): Renewal.
- Paristēmi (παρίστημι): To present, yield.
- o   Panim (פָּנִים): Presence, face.
- Hagios (ἅγιος): Holy, set apart.

CHAPTER 4

Kingdom Mindset Renewal: Foundations for Kingdom Living

Introduction: The Call to a Transformed Mindset

Every Kingdom citizen begins and continues their journey in Christ through the renewal of the mind. The Kingdom of God is not built upon religious rituals, denominational traditions, or cultural preferences but upon revelation that reshapes how we think, believe, and live. A renewed mind is not an accessory to Kingdom living—it is the foundation. Without it, we cannot properly perceive God's will, discern His truth, or live out His purposes.

Paul makes this central when he writes:

> *"I appeal to you therefore, brothers, by the mercies of God, to present your bodies as a living sacrifice, holy and acceptable to God, which is your spiritual worship. Do not be conformed to this world, but be transformed by the renewal of your mind, that by testing you may discern what is the will of God, what is good and acceptable and perfect."*
>
> Romans 12:1–2

The Greek word for mind, nous (νοῦς), refers to the faculty of perception, understanding, and moral reasoning. The word for renewal, anakainōsis (ἀνακαίνωσις), means renovation, complete change for the better. Together, Paul is declaring that Kingdom living requires a radical reorientation of thought, perception, and reasoning. We cannot enter into Kingdom reality with worldly mindsets.

Mindset as the Battlefront

The greatest spiritual battles are waged in the mind. Satan blinds, deceives, and distorts at the level of thought. Paul describes this vividly:

> *"In their case the god of this world has blinded the minds of the unbelievers, to keep them from seeing the light of the gospel of the glory of Christ, who is the image of God."*
>
> 2 Corinthians 4:4

The Greek word for blinded here, typhloō (τυφλόω), means to make blind, to obscure vision. This is more than physical blindness—it is spiritual disorientation, a mind unable to perceive truth. A mind blinded by delusion cannot see the Kingdom clearly.

This is why renewing the mind is essential. It is not enough to change external behaviors while internal thinking remains worldly. Israel in the wilderness is a case study. Though they were delivered physically from Egypt, their minds were still enslaved. They longed for the food of Egypt, resisted God's commands, and doubted His promises. God brought them out of bondage, but they had not yet let Egypt out of their minds.

> *"And the people of Israel said to them, 'Would that we had died by the hand of the Lord in the land of Egypt, when we sat by the meat pots and ate bread to the full, for you have brought us out into this wilderness to kill this whole assembly with hunger.'"*
>
> *Exodus 16:3*

Deliverance without renewal results in rebellion. The old mindset cannot carry new covenant promises.

Repentance as the First Step

The entry point into Kingdom mindset renewal is repentance. Jesus begins His ministry with this command:

> *"From that time Jesus began to preach, saying, 'Repent, for the kingdom of heaven is at hand.'"*
>
> *Matthew 4:17*

The Greek word metanoia (μετάνοια) means more than sorrow; it means a complete change of mind and direction. It comes from meta ("after, beyond") and nous ("mind, perception"). Repentance is not simply feeling sorry—it is thinking differently, aligning one's mind with God's truth.

Repentance dethrones self and enthrones God. It dismantles delusion and opens the heart to revelation. Without repentance, the mind remains clouded, and the Kingdom remains inaccessible.

The Pattern of This World vs. the Mind of Christ

Paul warns against being conformed to this world. The word syschēmatizō (συσχηματίζω) means to be pressed into a mold, to adopt the pattern of external culture. Worldly conformity enslaves us to trends, ideologies, and pressures. Kingdom renewal resists this by adopting the mind of Christ.

> *"Have this mind among yourselves, which is yours in Christ Jesus, who, though he was in the form of God, did not count equality with God a thing to be grasped, but emptied himself, by taking the form of a servant, being born in the likeness of men."*
>
> Philippians 2:5–7

The mind of Christ (phroneō – φρονέω, "to think, to set one's mind on") is humility, surrender, and service. It is not self-exaltation but self-emptying. Kingdom mindset renewal means we view ourselves, others, and our mission through the lens of Christ's humility and obedience.

Paul's Transformation:

A Case Study

Paul himself embodies the power of renewal of mindset. Once, Saul, zealous in persecuting the Church, encountered revelation on the Damascus road.

> *"Now, as he went on his way, he approached Damascus, and suddenly a light from heaven shone around him. And falling to the ground he heard a voice saying to him, 'Saul, Saul, why are you persecuting me?' And he said, 'Who are you, Lord?' And he said, 'I am Jesus, whom you are persecuting.'"*
>
> *Acts 9:3–5*

Saul's worldview was shattered. The persecutor of Christ became the apostle of Christ. His mind was renewed not by argument but by revelation. He later testified:

> *"But whatever gain I had, I counted as loss for the sake of Christ. Indeed, I count everything as loss because of the surpassing worth of knowing Christ Jesus my Lord."*
>
> *Philippians 3:7–8*

Renewal transformed Paul's values, priorities, and mission. This is the essence of Kingdom mindset renewal: reorienting all of life around Christ and His Kingdom.

The Early Church: A Renewed Community

The book of Acts records the early Church as a community marked by renewed minds and transformed priorities.

> *"And they devoted themselves to the apostles' teaching and the fellowship, to the breaking of bread and the prayers. And awe came upon every soul, and many wonders and signs were being done through the apostles. And all who believed were together and had all things in common. And they were selling their possessions and belongings and distributing the proceeds to all, as any had need."*
>
> *Acts 2:42–45*

Their devotion to teaching (didachē – διδαχή), fellowship (koinōnia – κοινωνία), and prayer produced a culture of generosity, unity, and power. Their renewed mindset led to renewed community. They were no longer driven by self-interest but by Kingdom priorities.

Modern Parallels: Cultural Mindsets and Identity Confusion

Today, many struggle to live Kingdom lives because they are still bound by cultural mindsets. Consumerism, individualism, nationalism, and relativism press us into molds contrary to Kingdom truth. When our identity is shaped more by social media, politics, or tradition than by revelation, our minds remain unrenewed.

Identity confusion arises when we define ourselves by race, class, denomination, or preference rather than by Christ. Paul rebukes this in the Corinthian church:

> *"For when one says, 'I follow Paul,' and another, 'I follow Apollos,' are you not being merely human? What then is Apollos? What is Paul? Servants through whom you believed, as the Lord assigned to each."*
>
> 1 Corinthians 3:4–5

Renewal shifts us from human allegiance to Kingdom allegiance. It restores identity as sons and daughters of God rather than as members of factions.

The Role of the Spirit in Renewal

Mindset renewal is the work of the Holy Spirit. Paul writes:

> *"And we all, with unveiled face, beholding the glory of the Lord, are being transformed into the same image from one degree of glory to another. For this comes from the Lord who is the Spirit."*
>
> 2 Corinthians 3:18

The Spirit unveils, reveals, and transforms. Renewal is not self-help but Spirit-help. As we behold Christ, the Spirit reshapes our thinking, refines our desires, and realigns our worldview.

Practical Pathways to Renewed Thinking

- ✔ Scripture Saturation: The Word of God renews by confronting lies with truth.

- ✔ Prayerful Surrender: Renewal requires yielding daily to God's presence.
- ✔ Worship Lifestyle: Worship reorients priorities around God's worthiness.
- ✔ Community Accountability: Fellowship with mature believers sharpens thinking.
- ✔ Discernment Practice: Testing every idea against Scripture guards against delusion.

Conclusion: The Mindset of Kingdom Citizens

Renewal of the mind is foundational for Kingdom living. Without it, we are conformed to the world. With it, we discern God's will, embody His presence, and live as transformed citizens of His Kingdom. This is not optional; it is the only way forward. To walk in the Kingdom is to think differently, to see differently, and to live differently. The renewed mind is the renewed life.

Glossary of Key Terms

- Nous (νοῦς): Mind, perception, understanding.
- Anakainōsis (ἀνακαίνωσις): Renewal, renovation.
- Typhloō (τυφλόω): To blind, obscure vision.
- Metanoia (μετάνοια): Repentance, change of mind.
- Syschēmatizō (συσχηματίζω): To conform, assume outward form.
- Phroneō (φρονέω): To think, set one's mind on.
- Didachē (διδαχή): Teaching, doctrine.
- Koinōnia (κοινωνία): Fellowship, partnership.
- Paristēmi (παρίστημι): To present, yield.
- Huiothesia (υἱοθεσία): Adoption, placement as sons.

CHAPTER 5

Ancient Israel's Watchmen – Prophets, Priests, and Gatekeepers

Introduction: Guardians of Covenant Life

Ancient Israel understood that survival, identity, and faithfulness to God required more than strong armies or fertile land. Their greatest strength lay in their covenant relationship with Yahweh. To protect this covenant life, God appointed watchmen—prophets, priests, and gatekeepers who stood as guardians of His people. These roles were not ceremonial; they were essential. Without watchmen, Israel drifted into idolatry. Without priests, holiness was compromised. Without gatekeepers, the city and Temple were vulnerable. Together, these offices embodied vigilance, discernment, and accountability. They safeguarded not only physical boundaries but also spiritual fidelity.

The Hebrew word shamar (שָׁמַר) means "to keep, guard, watch, preserve." It appears more than 460 times in the Old Testament, revealing the centrality of watchfulness in covenant life. Israel's watchmen were called to shamar the people of God, ensuring that His presence remained among them. This was not a passive assignment but an active duty requiring clarity, courage, and consecration.

Prophets: Voices of Revelation and Warning

Prophets functioned as Israel's spiritual watchmen. Their task was to hear from God and declare His word, often against cultural drift and spiritual complacency.

> *"So you, son of man, I have made a watchman for the house of Israel. Whenever you hear a word from my mouth, you shall give them warning from me."*
>
> *Ezekiel 33:7*

The Hebrew word for prophet, nabi (נָבִיא), means "one who is called or appointed to speak." The prophet did not speak his own opinion; he echoed the voice of God. Ezekiel, Jeremiah, and Isaiah stood in this office, often rejected by their own people yet faithful to their charge.

Jeremiah lamented the stubbornness of Israel's delusion:

> *"From the least to the greatest of them, everyone is greedy for unjust gain; and from prophet to priest, everyone deals falsely. They have healed the wound of my people lightly, saying, 'Peace, peace,' when there is no peace."*
>
> *Jeremiah 6:13–14*

The prophets exposed sin, confronted delusion, and called for repentance. Their watchman role was both protective and corrective, ensuring that God's people were not lulled into false security.

Priests: Guardians of Holiness

The priestly office was central to Israel's covenant identity. Priests mediated between God and the people, teaching the law, offering sacrifices, and maintaining holiness.

> *"For the lips of a priest should guard knowledge, and people should seek instruction from his mouth, for he is the messenger of the Lord of hosts."*
>
> *Malachi 2:7*

The Hebrew word kohen (כֹּהֵן) means priest, one who stands to serve in sacred duty. Priests guarded access to God's presence by ensuring the purity of offerings and teaching the law faithfully. Their negligence invited judgment, as in the days of Eli when corruption in the priesthood led to God's glory departing from Israel (1 Samuel 2–4).

Priests carried the responsibility of holiness. The Greek New Testament equivalent, hiereus (ἱερεύς), is used of Jesus as the great High Priest who offers Himself as the final sacrifice (Hebrews 7). As guardians of holiness, priests illustrated the principle that access to God requires purity and consecration.

Gatekeepers: Protectors of Presence

Beyond prophets and priests, Israel also appointed gatekeepers. These men guarded the entrances to the city and Temple, ensuring that only those qualified could enter.

> *"The gatekeepers were on the four sides, east, west, north, and south. And their kinsmen who were in their villages were obligated to come in every seven days, in turn, to be with these, for the four chief gatekeepers, who were Levites, were entrusted to be over the chambers and the treasures of the house of God."*
>
> *1 Chronicles 9:24–26*

The Hebrew word shoer (שֹׁעֵר) means gatekeeper, doorkeeper. These Levites were not simply guards; they were protectors of God's holy presence. Their vigilance prevented defilement and maintained the sanctity of worship. Nehemiah, when rebuilding Jerusalem's walls, prioritized the appointment of gatekeepers to secure the city physically and spiritually (Nehemiah 7:1).

Gatekeepers embodied the principle that not everything and everyone belongs within the sacred. They remind us that discernment and boundaries are vital in preserving God's presence among His people.

Case Study: Samuel as Prophet and Priest

Samuel represents the convergence of prophetic and priestly roles. Raised in the tabernacle, he ministered as a priest, yet he also functioned as a prophet who delivered God's word faithfully.

> *"And Samuel grew, and the Lord was with him and let none of his words fall to the ground. And all Israel from Dan to Beersheba knew that Samuel was established as a prophet of the Lord."*
>
> 1 Samuel 3:19–20

Samuel watched over Israel in a time of transition, guiding them from the corruption of Eli's priesthood to the anointing of kings. His watchman role preserved Israel's identity and redirected them toward God's covenant faithfulness.

Case Study: Nehemiah's Gatekeepers

After the exile, Nehemiah understood that rebuilding the walls was insufficient. Without gatekeepers, the city remained vulnerable.

> *"Now when the wall had been built and I had set up the doors, and the gatekeepers, the singers, and the Levites had been appointed, I gave my brother Hanani and Hananiah the governor of the castle charge over Jerusalem, for he was a more faithful and God-fearing man than many."*
>
> Nehemiah 7:1–2

Nehemiah's prioritization of gatekeepers reveals the importance of spiritual as well as physical protection. Faithfulness and fear of God were the qualifications for those who guarded the gates. Without faithful watchmen, the city's defenses would crumble from within.

The Watchman Mandate Today

While prophets, priests, and gatekeepers were specific offices in Israel, the watchman mandate continues in the Kingdom of God. Today, pastors, teachers, intercessors, and spiritual leaders stand as watchmen over God's people. Paul modeled this when he declared:

> *"Therefore, I testify to you this day that I am innocent of the blood of all, for I did not shrink from declaring to you the whole counsel of God. Pay careful attention to yourselves and to all the flock, in which the Holy Spirit has made you overseers, to care for the church of God, which he obtained with his own blood."*
>
> Acts 20:26–28

The Greek word episkopos (ἐπίσκοπος) means overseer, guardian. Paul understood his role as a spiritual watchman accountable to God for faithfully warning, teaching, and protecting the flock.

Today's watchmen must confront false teaching, guard against cultural drift, and preserve the holiness of God's people. They must also function as gatekeepers, discerning what enters the life of the community. In an age of open access, digital influence, and widespread deception, the role of spiritual gatekeepers is more urgent than ever.

Holiness, Presence, and Accountability

The common thread uniting prophets, priests, and gatekeepers is their commitment to holiness, presence, and accountability. Prophets declared the word of God. Priests maintained the purity of worship. Gatekeepers protected the sanctity of God's dwelling. Each role emphasized vigilance—watching, guarding, preserving.

he Hebrew shamar ties these roles together. To shamar is to guard covenant faithfulness. This is why God commanded Adam to "keep" the garden (Genesis 2:15). Humanity's first assignment was watchfulness, and its failure led to the fall. The Kingdom mandate of watchmen is thus a restoration of our original purpose: to guard the presence of God in our midst.

Modern Parallels and Application

The Church today needs prophets who boldly proclaim truth, priests who live holy and mediate God's presence, and gatekeepers who guard against compromise. Without them, communities drift into delusion, idolatry, and irrelevance.

Prophets today are voices of clarity in a culture of noise. They speak God's truth without compromise, even when unpopular.

Priests today embody holiness in daily life, modeling consecration and guiding others in worship and discipleship.

Gatekeepers today are intercessors, leaders, and elders who guard the community's spiritual health, discerning influences and protecting boundaries.

The modern watchman mandate requires courage. In a world of blurred lines, watchmen must be willing to call sin sin, to expose deception, and to uphold truth. Their vigilance preserves covenant life and ensures that the presence of God remains central.

Conclusion: The Enduring Call of the Watchman

Ancient Israel's prophets, priests, and gatekeepers remind us that watchfulness is not optional; it is essential. Without them, covenant identity crumbled, worship was corrupted, and communities were vulnerable. With them, the people of God were preserved, corrected, and led into faithfulness.

Today, the Church is called to continue this legacy. Every leader, every disciple, every intercessor is summoned to the watchman mandate. We are to guard the truth, protect holiness, and preserve the presence of God among His people. The Kingdom requires vigilance. To neglect the watchman's call is to invite drift and delusion. To embrace it is to secure transformation and identity for generations

Glossary of Key Terms

- Shamar (שָׁמַר): To keep, guard, watch, preserve.
- Nabi (נָבִיא): Prophet, one appointed to speak God's word.
- Kohen (כֹּהֵן): Priest, one who mediates and serves in holiness.
- Hiereus (ἱερεύς): Greek for priest, used of Jesus as High Priest.
- Shoer (שֹׁעֵר): Gatekeeper, doorkeeper.
- Phylax (φύλαξ): Greek for guard, watchman.
- Episkopos (ἐπίσκοπος): Overseer, guardian.
- Shamar Mandate: The responsibility to guard covenant faithfulness and God's presence.

CHAPTER 6

The Kingdom Call to Holiness and Distinction

Introduction: A People Set Apart

From the beginning, God's call upon His people has been one of separation, consecration, and distinction. Holiness is not an accessory to the life of faith; it is the essence of what it means to belong to the King. The Kingdom of God cannot be understood apart from the call to be a people set apart, reflecting His character in a world bent on compromise.

"You shall be holy, for I the Lord your God am holy."

Leviticus 19:2

The Hebrew word for holy, qadosh (קָדוֹשׁ), means "set apart, consecrated, distinct, other." Holiness is not first about behavior but about belonging. To be holy is to be separated unto God for His purposes. This separation creates distinction—visible evidence that a people belong to God and not to themselves or the surrounding culture.

The New Testament continues this theme with the Greek word hagios (ἅγιος), meaning "holy, set apart." Believers are called "saints" (hagioi), not because of perfection but because of their consecration to God. Holiness is not optional; it is identity. Distinction is not elitism; it is witness. Together, holiness and distinction are the marks of Kingdom citizenship.

Holiness as God's Original Intent

Creation itself reveals God's design for holiness. Humanity was created in God's image to reflect His nature (Genesis 1:27). The fall fractured this holiness, replacing purity with corruption, but God's intent never changed. From Eden to Sinai, from the prophets to Christ, the call to holiness has remained consistent.

> *"For I am the Lord who brought you up out of the land of Egypt to be your God. You shall therefore be holy, for I am holy."*
>
> *Leviticus 11:45*

Holiness is relational before it is behavioral. God delivered Israel so that they might be His own people. The Hebrew verb qadash (קָדַשׁ) means "to sanctify, to consecrate, to dedicate." God sanctifies His people by drawing them into a covenant with Himself. Their response is to live in distinction, refusing to conform to the nations around them.

Distinction as Covenant Identity

Israel's laws were not arbitrary. They were markers of distinction—daily reminders that Israel was not like the nations.

> *"You are a people holy to the Lord your God. The Lord your God has chosen you to be a people for his treasured possession, out of all the peoplescface of the earth."*
>
> *Deuteronomy 7:6*

The Hebrew word for treasured possession, segullah (סְגֻלָּה), means a private, prized treasure. Israel's dietary laws, sabbath observances, and purity codes were not about legalism but about reinforcing identity. Distinction was the visual evidence of holiness.

This principle continues in the New Testament. Peter echoes the language of Exodus when he declares:

> *"But you are a chosen race, a royal priesthood, a holy nation, a people for his own possession, that you may proclaim the excellencies of him who called you out of darkness into his marvelous light."*
>
> *1 Peter 2:9*

The Greek word for possession, peripoiēsis (περιποίησις), means "to acquire, preserve, or treasure." Kingdom distinction is not prideful separation; it is purposeful proclamation. God sets us apart so that we might display His excellencies in the world.

Case Study: Israel in the Wilderness

Israel's wilderness journey reveals the tension between holiness and compromise. Though delivered from Egypt, they often longed for Egypt's familiarity.

> *"We remember the fish we ate in Egypt that cost nothing, the cucumbers, the melons, the leeks, the onions, and the garlic. But now our strength is dried up, and there is nothing at all but this manna to look at."*
>
> *Numbers 11:5–6*

Israel's appetite betrayed their lack of holiness. Holiness requires desiring God above former attachments. The manna represented dependence on God, but Israel craved Egypt's abundance. Distinction cannot be maintained when appetites are tethered to the past.

Their failure to enter the promised land was not due to God's lack of provision but their refusal to embrace holiness. As

Hebrews reminds us:

> *"So we see that they were unable to enter because of unbelief."*
>
> *Hebrews 3:19*

Holiness and faith are inseparable. To be holy is to trust God's provision, presence, and promises over cultural enticements.

Case Study: Daniel in Babylon

Daniel illustrates the power of holiness in exile. Taken into Babylonian captivity, Daniel resolved not to defile himself with the king's food.

> *"But Daniel resolved that he would not defile himself with the king's food, or with the wine that he drank. Therefore he asked the chief of the eunuchs to allow him not to defile himself."*
>
> *Daniel 1:8*

The Hebrew word for defile, ga'al (גָּאַל), means "to pollute, stain, make ceremonially unclean." Daniel's refusal was not about food preferences but about holiness. His distinction preserved his witness and led to God's favor.

Daniel's holiness distinguished him not only from Babylonian culture but also among his peers. His uncompromising faith led to divine wisdom, influence in government, and miraculous deliverance. Holiness became the foundation of his leadership and legacy.

Holiness in the Teachings of Jesus

Jesus intensified the call to holiness by addressing the heart.

> *"You therefore must be perfect, as your heavenly Father is perfect."*
>
> Matthew 5:48

The Greek word teleios (τέλειος) means complete, mature, whole. Jesus was not demanding flawlessness but wholeness—a life fully aligned with the Father's character. Holiness is not about external compliance but internal transformation.

In John 17, Jesus prays for His disciples:

> *"Sanctify them in the truth; your word is truth. As you sent me into the world, so I have sent them into the world. And for their sake I consecrate myself, that they also may be sanctified in truth."*
>
> John 17:17–19

The Greek word hagiasmos (ἁγιασμός) means sanctification, the process of being made holy. Jesus consecrates Himself so that His people may be sanctified. Holiness is thus rooted in Christ's work and extended by the Spirit.

The Early Church: A Holy Witness

The early church carried the call to holiness into their communities. They were marked by generosity, purity, and bold witness. Ananias and Sapphira serve as a sobering example of what happens when holiness is compromised.

> *"But Peter said, 'Ananias, why has Satan filled your heart to lie to the Holy Spirit and to keep back for yourself part of the proceeds of the land? ... You have not lied to man but to God.' When Ananias heard these words, he fell down and breathed his last."*
>
> *Acts 5:3–5*

The early church understood that holiness was not optional. Distinction was not merely cultural but spiritual. Their fear of the Lord preserved their witness and expanded their influence.

Holiness and Identity Mapping

Holiness is inseparable from identity. In Christ, believers are called saints (hagioi). This is not an honorary title but a present reality. Our identity is holy because our King is holy.

Paul emphasizes this in his letters:

> *"To the church of God that is in Corinth, to those sanctified in Christ Jesus, called to be saints together with all those who in every place call upon the name of our Lord Jesus Christ, both their Lord and ours."*
>
> *1 Corinthians 1:2*

Sanctification is both positional and progressive. In Christ, we are already sanctified; in practice, we are being sanctified. The Greek word hagiazō (ἁγιάζω) means "to make holy, to consecrate." Identity mapping in the Kingdom begins with this reality: we are holy, and therefore we live holy.

Distinction as Witness in the World

Holiness is not withdrawal from the world but distinction within it. Jesus prayed not that His disciples would be taken out of the world but that they would be kept from evil (John 17:15). Distinction means living differently within the same environment.

Paul writes:

> "Therefore go out from their midst, and be separate from them, says the Lord, and touch no unclean thing; then I will welcome you, and I will be a father to you, and you shall be sons and daughters to me, says the Lord Almighty."
>
> 2 Corinthians 6:17–18

The Greek word aphorizō (ἀφορίζω) means to mark off by boundaries, to separate. Distinction establishes boundaries that protect holiness and witness.

In a culture that blurs lines, Kingdom citizens must embrace clarity. Distinction in speech, ethics, relationships, and priorities reveals the reality of God's Kingdom. Holiness becomes evangelism when lived consistently.

Modern Parallels: Holiness in a Compromised Age

Today's church faces pressures similar to Israel in the wilderness and Daniel in Babylon. Consumerism, relativism, and secularism tempt believers to compromise. Yet the call to holiness remains unchanged.

- ✔ Holiness in relationships resists sexual immorality and embraces covenant faithfulness.
- ✔ Holiness in economics rejects greed and embraces generosity.
- ✔ Holiness in speech resists corruption and embraces truth.
- ✔ Holiness in worship resists entertainment and embraces reverence.
- ✔ Holiness is countercultural, but it is also transformative. It distinguishes Kingdom citizens in a world desperate for authenticity.

Conclusion: The King's Holy Nation

The Kingdom call to holiness and distinction is not a burden but a privilege. To be holy is to belong to God. To be distinct is to display His excellencies in the world. Holiness preserves identity, empowers witness, and sustains presence.

"Strive for peace with everyone, and for the holiness without which no one will see the Lord."

Hebrews 12:14

The Greek word diōkō (διώκω) means to pursue earnestly. Holiness requires intentional pursuit. Distinction requires vigilance. Together, they form the foundation of Kingdom living.

As Kingdom citizens, we must embrace the privilege of being set apart. We are not called to blend in but to stand out—not for our glory but for His. Holiness is our identity. Distinction is our testimony. Together, they declare to the world that the King reigns.

Glossary of Key Terms

- Qadosh (קָדוֹשׁ): Holy, set apart, consecrated.
- Qadash (קָדַשׁ): To sanctify, dedicate, consecrate.
- Segullah (סְגֻלָּה): Treasured possession.
- Hagios (ἅγιος): Holy, set apart.
- Hagioi (ἅγιοι): Saints, holy ones.
- Hagiasmos (ἁγιασμός): Sanctification, process of being made holy.
- Hagiazō (ἁγιάζω): To make holy, to consecrate.
- o Teleios (τέλειος): Perfect, complete, mature.
- Ga'al (גָּאַל): To defile, pollute.
- Aphorizō (ἀφορίζω): To separate, mark off boundaries.
- Peripoiēsis (περιποίησις): Possession, treasure.

CHAPTER 7

Covenant Faithfulness and Kingdom Continuity

Introduction: The God Who Keeps Covenant

At the very heart of Scripture is the reality that God is a covenant-making and covenant-keeping God. From Genesis to Revelation, the thread that ties God's Kingdom purposes together is His faithfulness to the covenant. He binds Himself to His people, not because they are flawless, but because He is faithful. His Kingdom cannot be separated from His covenant promises. To understand Kingdom continuity across generations, we must grasp God's covenantal nature.

> *"Know therefore that the Lord your God is God, the faithful God who keeps covenant and steadfast love with those who love him and keep his commandments, to a thousand generations."*
>
> *Deuteronomy 7:9*

The Hebrew word for covenant, berith (בְּרִית), comes from a root meaning "to cut." It refers to a solemn agreement sealed by sacrifice. Covenant is not casual; it is costly. God's faithfulness to berith reveals His steadfast love (chesed – חֶסֶד), His loyal commitment to His people. In the New Testament, the Greek word diathēkē (διαθήκη) carries this meaning of covenant or testament, pointing to God's binding commitment fulfilled in Christ.

God's covenant faithfulness is the foundation of Kingdom continuity. His purposes do not shift with cultural trends or human failure. What He establishes by covenant, He sustains by His own faithfulness.

The Covenant with Noah: Preserving Creation

After the flood, God established a covenant with Noah as a sign of His commitment to preserve creation.

> "I establish my covenant with you, that never again shall all flesh be cut off by the waters of the flood, and never again shall there be a flood to destroy the earth. And God said, 'This is the sign of the covenant that I make between me and you and every living creature that is with you, for all future generations: I have set my bow in the cloud, and it shall be a sign of the covenant between me and the earth.'"
>
> Genesis 9:11–13

The rainbow (qeshet – קֶשֶׁת) symbolized God's promise to preserve life. This covenant revealed God's mercy and His desire for continuity. Even in judgment, God bound Himself to creation in faithfulness.

The Abrahamic Covenant: Kingdom Seed and Promise

With Abraham, God revealed the covenant as the means of blessing the nations.

> *"And I will make of you a great nation, and I will bless you and make your name great, so that you will be a blessing. I will bless those who bless you, and him who dishonors you I will curse, and in you all the families of the earth shall be blessed."*
>
> *Genesis 12:2–3*

Here, Berith takes on a missional dimension. God's covenant with Abraham was not merely for one family but for all nations. The covenant required faith—pistis (πίστις) in the Greek New Testament sense—trust in God's promises despite present impossibility. Abraham believed God, and it was counted to him as righteousness (Genesis 15:6; Romans 4:3).

The Abrahamic covenant reveals Kingdom continuity through faith. Abraham's descendants became Israel, but the ultimate seed was Christ (Galatians 3:16). In Christ, the blessing extends to all nations, fulfilling the covenant's scope.

The Sinai Covenant: A Holy Nation

At Sinai, God formed Israel into a covenant nation.

> *"Now therefore, if you will indeed obey my voice and keep my covenant, you shall be my treasured possession among all peoples, for all the earth is mine; and you shall be to me a kingdom of priests and a holy nation."*
>
> *Exodus 19:5–6*

The Hebrew word for treasured possession, segullah (סְגֻלָּה), emphasizes Israel's distinct identity. Covenant at Sinai provided laws, rituals, and structures that set Israel apart. It demanded obedience as the response to grace.

Yet Israel repeatedly broke the covenant. Prophets like Hosea portrayed this as spiritual adultery. God's people betrayed His faithfulness, but He remained loyal. Chesed, covenant love, sustained continuity even in exile. Jeremiah declared:

> *"Behold, the days are coming, declares the Lord, when I will make a new covenant with the house of Israel and the house of Judah."*
>
> *Jeremiah 31:31*

Even in failure, the covenant pointed forward to fulfillment.

The Davidic Covenant: Kingdom Continuity through a Throne

God's covenant with David established the continuity of His Kingdom through an everlasting throne.

> *"Your house and your kingdom shall be made sure forever before me. Your throne shall be established forever."*
>
> *2 Samuel 7:16*

The Hebrew word olam (עוֹלָם) means eternal, perpetual. Though David sinned, God's covenant endured. The Davidic covenant pointed directly to Christ, the Son of David, who reigns eternally. Matthew's genealogy and Luke's gospel both emphasize this continuity: Jesus is the promised King whose throne fulfills covenant faithfulness.

The New Covenant in Christ: Fulfillment and Transformation

The climax of covenant history is the new covenant in Christ.

> *"And he took bread, and when he had given thanks, he broke it and gave it to them, saying, 'This is my body, which is given for you. Do this in remembrance of me.' And likewise the cup after they had eaten, saying, 'This cup that is poured out for you is the new covenant in my blood."*
>
> *Luke 22:19–20*

The Greek phrase hē kainē diathēkē (ἡ καινὴ διαθήκη) means "the new covenant." Jesus' blood sealed this covenant, fulfilling Jeremiah's prophecy. Unlike the old covenant written on stone, the new covenant writes God's law on hearts (Jeremiah 31:33). It provides forgiveness, transformation, and the indwelling Spirit.

Paul explains:

> *"Such is the confidence that we have through Christ toward God. Not that we are sufficient in ourselves to claim anything as coming from us, but our sufficiency is from God, who has made us competent to be ministers of a new covenant, not of the letter but of the Spirit. For the letter kills, but the Spirit gives life."*
>
> *2 Corinthians 3:4–6*

Kingdom continuity flows through this covenant, transforming individuals and forming a people marked by Spirit-empowered holiness.

Covenant Faithfulness and Generational Continuity

Covenant is not limited to individuals; it spans generations. God describes Himself as faithful "to a thousand generations" (Deuteronomy 7:9). Abraham's faith blessed Isaac and Jacob. David's covenant pointed to Christ centuries later. Continuity depends not on human perfection but on God's steadfastness.

This continuity demands faithful stewardship. Parents are called to pass the covenant faith to children. Leaders are called to guard covenant truth for their communities. Paul modeled this in his discipleship of Timothy:

> *"What you have heard from me in the presence of many witnesses entrust to faithful men who will be able to teach others also."*
>
> 2 Timothy 2:2

Here we see four generations of continuity—Paul, Timothy, faithful men, and others. Covenant faithfulness ensures Kingdom expansion across time.

Modern Parallels:

- ✔ Covenant in Community and Leadership
- ✔ Today, covenant remains the framework of Kingdom continuity.

- ✔ Marriage reflects covenant faithfulness (Ephesians 5:22–33). Husbands and wives embody Christ and the Church in their commitment.
- ✔ Church membership is covenantal, not contractual. Believers are bound together in love and accountability, reflecting God's covenant loyalty.
- ✔ Leadership in the Kingdom requires covenant fidelity. Leaders are not hirelings but shepherds entrusted with covenant stewardship.
- ✔ Discipleship is covenantal formation—passing on truth, guarding identity, and sustaining continuity.

Without a covenant, the Church drifts into consumerism and fragmentation. With the covenant, the Church reflects God's faithfulness and continuity.

The God Who Cannot Fail

Ultimately, covenant continuity rests not on human strength but on God's unchanging nature.

> *"If we are faithless, he remains faithful—for he cannot deny himself."*
>
> *2 Timothy 2:13*

The Greek word pistos (πιστός) means faithful, trustworthy. God's faithfulness is self-grounded. His covenant endures because His character is unchanging.

Revelation shows the final covenant fulfillment:

> *"And I heard a loud voice from the throne saying, 'Behold, the dwelling place of God is with man. He will dwell with them, and they will be his people, and God himself will be with them as their God. He will wipe away every tear from their eyes, and death shall be no more, neither shall there be mourning, nor crying, nor pain anymore, for the former things have passed away.'"*
>
> *Revelation 21:3–4*

This is covenant consummation—God with His people forever, continuity completed, faithfulness revealed.

Conclusion: Covenant as the Framework of the Kingdom

The Kingdom of God is covenantal. From Noah to Abraham, from Sinai to David, from Christ to the new creation, God has bound Himself to His people in faithfulness. Covenant is not an Old Testament relic but the framework of Kingdom continuity. It defines identity, sustains holiness, and ensures generational witness.

As Kingdom citizens, we must embrace the covenant as our foundation. Covenant faithfulness is not optional; it is the essence of belonging. Continuity is not automatic; it requires stewardship. But above all, the covenant rests on God's faithfulness, the God who cannot fail.

Glossary of Key Terms

- Berith (בְּרִית): Covenant, solemn agreement sealed by sacrifice.
- Chesed (חֶסֶד): Steadfast love, covenant loyalty.
- Diathēkē (διαθήκη): Covenant, testament.
- Pistis (πίστις): Faith, trust, faithfulness.
- Qeshet (קֶשֶׁת): Bow, rainbow, sign of covenant.
- Segullah (סְגֻלָּה): Treasured possession.
- Olam (עוֹלָם): Eternal, perpetual.
- Hē kainē diathēkē (ἡ καινὴ διαθήκη): The new covenant.
- Pistos (πιστός): Faithful, trustworthy

CHAPTER 8

Kingdom Culture and Influence:

The Mandate and Model for Kingdom Transformation

Introduction: Culture as the Arena of Kingdom Witness

Every generation must decide whether it will conform to the culture of the world or bear witness to the culture of the Kingdom. Culture is not neutral; it is the arena where values are shaped, identities are formed, and power is exercised. For Kingdom citizens, culture is both a mission field and a proving ground. God has called His people not to withdraw from culture nor to be consumed by it, but to transform it.

> *"You are the salt of the earth, but if salt has lost its taste, how shall its saltiness be restored? It is no longer good for anything except to be thrown out and trampled under people's feet. You are the light of the world. A city set on a hill cannot be hidden. Nor do people light a lamp and put it under a basket, but on a stand, and it gives light to all in the house. In the same way, let your light shine before others, so that they may see your good works and give glory to your Father who is in heaven."*
>
> *Matthew 5:13–16*

The Greek word for world, kosmos (κόσμος), refers not only to physical creation but to the ordered systems of human society. The Kingdom mandate is to function as salt (halas – ἅλας, a preserving agent) and light (phōs – φῶς, illumination and revelation) within the kosmos. Influence is not about domination but demonstration: showing forth God's character in every cultural sphere.

The Mandate of Kingdom Culture

God's covenant people were always intended to display His culture before the nations. Israel was called to be a "kingdom of priests and a holy nation" (Exodus 19:6), not merely for their own sake but as a witness to surrounding cultures.

> *"Keep them and do them, for that will be your wisdom and your understanding in the sight of the peoples, who, when they hear all these statutes, will say, 'Surely this great nation is a wise and understanding people.'"*
>
> *Deuteronomy 4:6*

The Hebrew word for wisdom, chokmah (חָכְמָה), implies skillful living—demonstrating God's character through practical obedience. Israel's distinct laws were not arbitrary; they were cultural markers of holiness that revealed Yahweh's wisdom. When Israel lived faithfully, they influenced the surrounding nations. When they compromised, they blended in and lost their witness.

The same is true for the Church. Our mandate is not to mimic the world's culture but to reveal Kingdom culture—a culture shaped by the reign of Christ.

Case Study: Daniel in Babylon

Daniel's story demonstrates Kingdom influence in a hostile culture. Though taken captive, Daniel resolved not to defile himself (Daniel 1:8). His holiness preserved his distinct identity, and God granted him favor and wisdom in Babylonian courts.

> *"As for these four youths, God gave them learning and skill in all literature and wisdom, and Daniel had understanding in all visions and dreams. And in every matter of wisdom and understanding about which the king inquired of them, he found them ten times better than all the magicians and enchanters that were in all his kingdom."*
>
> *Daniel 1:17, 20*

Daniel did not assimilate into Babylon's culture, yet he did not withdraw either. He engaged with Babylon's systems while maintaining covenant faithfulness. This balance is the model for Kingdom influence—engagement without compromise, witness without assimilation.

Case Study: Paul at Mars Hill

The apostle Paul provides another model of cultural engagement. In Athens, he observed altars to various gods, including one inscribed "To the unknown god." Instead of condemning their ignorance outright, Paul used it as a bridge to declare Christ.

> *"So Paul, standing in the midst of the Areopagus, said: 'Men of Athens, I perceive that in every way you are very religious. For as I passed along and observed the objects of your worship, I found also an altar with this inscription: "To the unknown god." What therefore you worship as unknown, this I proclaim to you.'"*
>
> *Acts 17:22–23*

The Greek word ethnos (ἔθνος) means nation or people group. Paul contextualized the gospel for the ethnos he was addressing, without diluting its truth. He quoted their poets (Acts 17:28) while pointing to Christ as the fulfillment of their searching. This demonstrates that

Kingdom culture can engage with human culture without being captured by it.

The Distinction of Kingdom Culture

What distinguishes Kingdom culture from worldly culture is its source. Worldly culture is shaped by human desires, power structures, and sin. Kingdom culture is shaped by God's reign, Spirit-empowered transformation, and holiness.

John warns:

> *"Do not love the world or the things in the world. If anyone loves the world, the love of the Father is not in him. For all that is in the world—the desires of the flesh and the desires of the eyes and pride of life—is not from the Father but is from the world. And the world is passing away along with its desires, but whoever does the will of God abides forever."*
>
> *1 John 2:15–17*

The Greek word epithymia (ἐπιθυμία) means inordinate desire, craving. Kingdom citizens must resist cultural cravings and instead embody Kingdom desires—righteousness, justice, and peace in the Holy Spirit (Romans 14:17).

Culture as the Arena of Transformation

Culture is where Kingdom transformation must be visible. Jesus declared the Kingdom to be like yeast that leavens the whole lump

(Matthew 13:33). The gospel is not content to remain private; it spreads, permeates, and transforms.

> *"Do not be conformed to this world, but be transformed by the renewal of your mind, that by testing you may discern what is the will of God, what is good and acceptable and perfect."*
>
> *Romans 12:2*

The Greek word metamorphoō (μεταμορφόω) means to transform, to change form. Culture is transformed not by coercion but by the visible witness of transformed lives. As Kingdom citizens live with renewed minds, they create new patterns of culture—families shaped by love, communities marked by justice, workplaces governed by integrity, governments influenced by righteousness.

Modern Parallels: The Battle of Cultures

Today's world presents competing cultural narratives. Secularism insists that faith should remain private. Consumerism teaches that identity comes from possessions. Relativism denies absolute truth. De-churching trends reveal that many prefer spirituality without submission to Christ's reign.

In this context, Kingdom culture must stand distinct. We cannot simply import worldly values into the Church and baptize them with religious language. Nor can we retreat into isolation. The mandate is to engage culture while revealing a higher order—the culture of the Kingdom.

- ✔ In education, Kingdom influence means raising truth-seekers, not consumers of information.
- ✔ In business, it means practicing integrity, generosity, and stewardship over greed.
- ✔ In politics, it means promoting justice rooted in God's character, not partisan agendas.
- ✔ In the arts, it means creating beauty that reflects God's glory rather than celebrating depravity.
- ✔ In families, it means covenantal love that resists fragmentation.

Kingdom culture transforms not by power plays but by persistent witness.

Influence flows from identity. When believers forget who they are, they forfeit their ability to shape culture. Jesus grounded influence in identity:

> *"You are the light of the world. A city set on a hill cannot be hidden."*
>
> *Matthew 5:14*

The verb eimi (εἰμί, "you are") emphasizes being, not doing. Influence is not first about strategy but about identity. Kingdom citizens influence culture because they embody Kingdom reality. Our identity as sons and daughters of God is the foundation of cultural transformation.

Conclusion: The Model for Kingdom Transformation

Kingdom culture and influence are not optional add-ons; they are the mandate of every believer. Culture is the arena of witness, the place where holiness meets the public square. The Church is not called to mirror culture but to model transformation.

"For once you were darkness, but now you are light in the Lord. Walk as children of light (for the fruit of light is found in all that is good and right and true), and try to discern what is pleasing to the Lord. Take no part in the unfruitful works of darkness, but instead expose them."

Ephesians 5:8–11

Kingdom culture is rooted in covenant identity, empowered by the Spirit, and expressed through holiness, justice, and love. The model for transformation is Christ Himself, who entered culture, engaged people, and revealed the Kingdom without compromise.

As His body, the Church continues that mission. To influence culture is to embody Kingdom values publicly. To transform culture is to demonstrate the reign of God in every sphere of life. This is the mandate and model of Kingdom transformation: to be in the world but not of it, to live as salt and light, and to reveal to all nations that the Kingdom of God has come.

Glossary of Key Terms

- Kosmos (κόσμος): World, ordered system of society.
- Ethnos (ἔθνος): Nation, people group.
- Basileia (βασιλεία): Kingdom, reign, rule.
- Phōs (φῶς): Light, illumination, revelation.
- Halas (ἅλας): Salt, preserving agent.
- Chokmah (חָכְמָה): Wisdom, skillful living.
- Epithymia (ἐπιθυμία): Desire, craving.
- Metamorphoō (μεταμορφόω): To transform, change form.
- Eimi (εἰμί): To be, to exist

CHAPTER 9

Kingdom Culture and Influence: The Mandate and Model for Kingdom Transformation

Introduction: Culture as the Arena of Kingdom Witness

Every Kingdom citizen must recognize that culture is never neutral. Culture is the arena where values are defined, power is exercised, and human identity is negotiated. It is also the arena where the Kingdom of God must bear witness to the reign of Christ. Our mandate is not to retreat from culture, nor to assimilate into it, but to engage, transform, and reorient culture around the truth of God's Kingdom.

> *"You are the salt of the earth, but if salt has lost its taste, how shall its saltiness be restored? It is no longer good for anything except to be thrown out and trampled under people's feet. You are the light of the world. A city set on a hill cannot be hidden. Nor do people light a lamp and put it under a basket, but on a stand, and it gives light to all in the house. In the same way, let your light shine before others, so that they may see your good works and give glory to your Father who is in heaven."*
>
> Matthew 5:13–16

The Greek word for "world," kosmos (κόσμος), refers to the ordered systems of human life and society. Jesus calls His disciples salt (halas – ἅλας, preservative, purifier) and light (phōs – φῶς, illumination, revelation). Kingdom citizens are designed to permeate culture, preserving it from decay and illuminating it with God's truth.

Kingdom Culture: Rooted in Covenant Identity

Culture is shaped by identity. A covenant relationship with Yahweh defined Israel's culture. Their laws, feasts, and worship practices set them apart from other nations.

> *"You are a people holy to the Lord your God. The Lord your God has chosen you to be a people for his treasured possession, out of all the peoples who are on the face of the earth."*
>
> *Deuteronomy 7:6*

The Hebrew word for "treasured possession," segullah (סְגֻלָּה), emphasizes belonging and value. Israel's distinct culture was not about elitism but about testimony. By living differently, they were to display the wisdom and holiness of God to surrounding nations.

> *"Keep them and do them, for that will be your wisdom and your understanding in the sight of the peoples, who, when they hear all these statutes, will say, 'Surely this great nation is a wise and understanding people.'"*
>
> *Deuteronomy 4:6*

God's Kingdom culture is thus rooted in covenant identity. As the Church, our witness is not found in mirroring cultural trends but in embodying covenant distinctiveness.

Case Study: Daniel in Babylon

Daniel's story is perhaps the clearest biblical example of cultural engagement without assimilation. Taken captive to Babylon, Daniel and his friends were pressured to adopt the Babylonian diet, education, and worship. Yet Daniel resolved not to defile himself.

> *"But Daniel resolved that he would not defile himself with the king's food, or with the wine that he drank. Therefore he asked the chief of the eunuchs to allow him not to defile himself."*
>
> *Daniel 1:8*

The Hebrew word ga'al (גָּאַל) means to defile or pollute. Daniel's distinction was not about rejecting knowledge—he learned Babylonian literature and wisdom—but about refusing to compromise holiness. His faithfulness led to favor, wisdom, and cultural influence.

Daniel demonstrates the model of Kingdom influence: engagement with culture without losing covenant identity.

Case Study: Paul at Mars Hill

The apostle Paul modeled cultural engagement in Athens. Rather than dismissing Greek religion, he observed their altars and used their own poetry as a bridge to proclaim Christ.

> *"So Paul, standing in the midst of the Areopagus, said: 'Men of Athens, I perceive that in every way you are very religious. For as I passed along and observed the objects of your worship, I found also an altar with this inscription: "To the unknown god." What therefore you worship as unknown, this I proclaim to you.'"*
>
> Acts 17:22–23

Paul contextualized the gospel without diluting its truth. He quoted their poets—"In him we live and move and have our being"—but reoriented their search for truth toward Christ. The Greek word ethnos (ἔθνος) points to nations, peoples. Paul engaged the ethnos with clarity and conviction, showing that Kingdom culture speaks into every human context.

The Distinction of Kingdom Culture

What makes Kingdom culture transformative is its source. While worldly culture is shaped by human desires, power, and sin, Kingdom culture flows from the reign of God. John warns:

> *"Do not love the world or the things in the world. If anyone loves the world, the love of the Father is not in him. For all that is in the world—the desires of the flesh and the desires of the eyes and pride of life—is not from the Father but is from the world. And the world is passing away along with its desires, but whoever does the will of God abides forever."*
>
> 1 John 2:15–17

The Greek word epithymia (ἐπιθυμία) refers to inordinate desire, craving. Worldly culture thrives on cravings, while Kingdom culture thrives on obedience. Holiness is the distinction that separates God's people from the cultural drift of the kosmos.

Modern Parallels: Competing Cultures in Today's World

Today's society mirrors Babylon and Athens—pluralistic, diverse, yet spiritually fragmented. Secularism insists that faith be privatized. Consumerism teaches that value is found in possessions. Political tribalism fractures communities, and digital media creates new idols of self-image and influence.

In digital culture, truth is often replaced by opinion. Kingdom citizens must embody integrity and discernment, not merely replicate online trends.

In politics, allegiance to parties often eclipses allegiance to Christ. Kingdom culture insists that justice is rooted in God's character, not partisan power.

In consumer culture, people are defined by what they buy rather than who they are. Kingdom influence reclaims identity as sons and daughters of God, not customers in an endless marketplace.

In secularized education, knowledge is divorced from wisdom. Kingdom culture restores knowledge as rooted in the fear of the Lord (Proverbs 9:10).

Kingdom citizens must resist assimilation while engaging culture faithfully. Influence flows not from imitation but from distinction.

Culture as the Arena of Transformation

Culture is transformed through the presence of Kingdom citizens. Jesus compared the Kingdom to leaven that spreads through dough:

> *"He told them another parable. 'The kingdom of heaven is like leaven that a woman took and hid in three measures of flour, till it was all leavened.'"*
>
> *Matthew 13:33*

The Greek word zymē (ζύμη) means yeast or leaven—small, yet transformative. Kingdom culture works quietly but persistently until it permeates every sphere. Families shaped by love, communities marked by justice, and economies rooted in stewardship all testify to leaven at work.

Transformation is not imposed but demonstrated. As Paul writes:

> *"Do not be conformed to this world, but be transformed by the renewal of your mind, that by testing you may discern what is the will of God, what is good and acceptable and perfect."*
>
> *Romans 12:2*

The Greek word metamorphoō (μεταμορφόω) indicates transformation from within. Kingdom culture transforms the kosmos through renewed minds that live differently.

Identity as the Foundation of Influence

Jesus ties cultural influence to identity.

"You are the light of the world. A city set on a hill cannot be hidden."

Matthew 5:14

The Greek verb eimi (εἰμί) means "to be." Influence flows from being, not from strategy. We do not need to manufacture Kingdom influence; we need to embody Kingdom identity. When we live as sons and daughters of God, we naturally reveal Kingdom culture in the world.

Conclusion: The Mandate and Model of Transformation

Kingdom culture and influence are not optional—they are the very mandate of discipleship. Culture is the proving ground of holiness, the arena of witness, and the platform of transformation. The Church must not mirror worldly culture but model Kingdom distinctiveness.

"For once you were darkness, but now you are light in the Lord. Walk as children of light (for the fruit of light is found in all that is good and right and true), and try to discern what is pleasing to the Lord. Take no part in the unfruitful works of darkness, but instead expose them."

Ephesians 5:8–11

The model is Christ Himself—engaged, incarnate, yet uncompromising. He entered human culture to redeem it, not to conform to it. As His body, we continue this mission: salt that preserves, light that illuminates, leaven that transforms.

Kingdom culture is both a mandate and a model. It is the call to embody holiness and the example of transformation for every generation. By embracing covenant identity and Spirit-empowered distinction, the Church becomes a cultural witness to the reign of God.

Glossary of Key Terms

- Kosmos (κόσμος): World, ordered system of society.
- Ethnos (ἔθνος): Nation, people group.
- Basileia (βασιλεία): Kingdom, reign, rule.
- Phōs (φῶς): Light, illumination, revelation.
- Halas (ἅλας): Salt, preservative.
- Chokmah (חָכְמָה): Wisdom, skillful living.
- Epithymia (ἐπιθυμία): Craving, inordinate desire.
- Metamorphoō (μεταμορφόω): To transform, change form.
- Zymē (ζύμη): Leaven, yeast, influence.
- Eimi (εἰμί): To be, essence of identity.

CHAPTER 10

Ethics and Justice: Embodying the King's Character in Kingdom Living

Introduction: The Weight of Kingdom Character

The Kingdom of God is the manifestation of the King's own nature in a people who bear His name. Ethics and justice are not accessories to Kingdom life; they are its substance. When we confess Jesus as Lord, we pledge to display His character in our motives, our relationships, our work, and our governance. Righteousness and justice are the foundation of His throne; therefore, they must become the framework of our conduct. The world reads the Gospel through the testimony of a just people. To live unjustly is to bear false witness about the King; to live justly is to reveal His reign.

> *"Righteousness and justice are the foundation of your throne; steadfast love and faithfulness go before you."*
>
> Psalm 89:14

The Foundation of Kingdom Ethics

In Scripture, righteousness and justice are covenant words. Tsedeq speaks to rightness aligned with God's ways; mishpat speaks to judgment, order, and fair practice among people. Together, they describe a life that reflects the King's nature privately and publicly. The New Testament gathers this union under dikaiosynē—righteousness-as-justice and justice-as-righteousness—erasing the false divide between personal piety and public responsibility. Kingdom ethics is not a set of human ideals; it is the outworking of the King's holy character in a covenant people.

> *"Blessed are those who hunger and thirst for righteousness, for they shall be satisfied."*
>
> *Matthew 5:6*

Justice as Covenant Faithfulness

Biblical justice is more than legal process; it is covenant faithfulness expressed toward neighbor, especially the vulnerable—the widow, the orphan, and the stranger. God's people do justice not to earn favor but because they have received covenant mercy. Justice is the shape mercy takes in public.

> *"He has told you, O man, what is good; and what does the Lord require of you but to do justice, to love mercy, and to walk humbly with your God?"*
>
> *Micah 6:8*

The Prophetic Demand for Integrity

The prophets rebuked worship that coexisted with exploitation. They insisted that songs and sacrifices are empty when scales are rigged, courts are partial, and laborers are defrauded. Their call reverberates today: holiness without justice is hypocrisy; justice without holiness is pride.

> *"Let justice roll down like waters, and righteousness like an ever-flowing stream."*
>
> Amos 5:24

> *"Learn to do good; seek justice, correct oppression; bring justice to the fatherless, plead the widow's cause."*
>
> Isaiah 1:17

The King as the Measure of Justice

Jesus embodies the Law and the Prophets. He intensifies the ethical vision: murder begins with anger, adultery with lust, false witness with oaths, and manipulative speech. He locates justice in the transformed heart that loves enemies, tells the truth without embellishment, and gives without show. His ministry announces liberty for the oppressed and good news to the poor. In Jesus, justice is restorative, not merely punitive; it aims at reconciliation and the recovery of image-bearers.

"Woe to you... for you tithe mint and dill and cumin, and have neglected the weightier matters of the law: justice and mercy and faithfulness."

Matthew 23:23

"The Spirit of the Lord is upon me... he has sent me to proclaim liberty to the captives... to set at liberty those who are oppressed."

Luke 4:18–19

The Apostolic Pattern

The apostles root ethics and justice in our life together. We put away falsehood and speak truth; we abandon theft and work so we may share; we lay down corrosive speech and put on words that build up. James declares that pure religion cares for the vulnerable and keeps unstained by the world. Peter exhorts us to live honorably before the nations so that our conduct answers slander. Paul forbids partiality and greed in leaders and instructs the church in equitable care for widows, fair wages, and integrity in business. The Spirit forms a people whose common life advertises the Kingdom.

> "Religion that is pure and undefiled before God the Father is this: to visit orphans and widows in their affliction, and to keep oneself unstained from the world."
>
> James 1:27

> "Repay no one evil for evil... If possible, so far as it depends on you, live peaceably with all."
>
> Romans 12:17–18

Case Study: Nathan Confronts David

David's abuse of power against Bathsheba and Uriah culminates in prophetic confrontation. Nathan's parable exposes a king who protected his image while destroying a home. True authority accepts truth, repents deeply, and seeks to repair. Psalm 51 demonstrates that justice begins in the heart, yet it does not end there; real repentance pursues restitution toward those harmed and renewed integrity in leadership.

> "Create in me a clean heart, O God, and renew a right spirit within me."
>
> Psalm 51:10

Case Study: Boaz, Ruth, and the Ethics of Provision

God commanded landowners to leave the edges of their fields for the poor and the foreigner. Boaz honors this law with generosity and protection, modeling employer ethics that combine lawful compliance with covenant kindness. Workplaces animated by Kingdom ethics create conditions where the vulnerable are shielded, dignified, and included.

> *"When you reap the harvest of your land, you shall not reap your field right up to its edge… you shall leave them for the poor and for the sojourner."*
>
> *Leviticus 19:9–10*

Case Study: Nehemiah and Economic Repentance

In Jerusalem's rebuilding, nobles charged interest that enslaved their brothers. Nehemiah calls an assembly, demands debt release, and requires a public oath. Justice here is structural: it addresses predatory systems, not only individual attitudes. Kingdom reform names exploitation, convenes the community, and enacts concrete policy that liberates.

> *"Let us abandon this exacting of interest. Return to them this very day their fields, their vineyards, their olive orchards, and their houses."*
>
> *Nehemiah 5:10–11*

Case Study: Daniel's Integrity in Imperial Systems

Daniel learns the language and literature of Babylon without surrendering holiness. He serves with excellence, refuses defilement, and prays though it costs him. Kingdom ethics engages institutions without assimilation. Influence grows from consecration coupled with competence.

> *"But Daniel resolved that he would not defile himself with the king's food."*
>
> *Daniel 1:8*

Case Study: Zacchaeus and the Practice of Restitution

Encounter with Jesus turns a dishonest tax collector into a just man who restores fourfold and gives to the poor. The sign of conversion is not mere sentiment but reparative action. Kingdom repentance includes financial integrity and practical repair of harms committed.

> *"Behold, Lord, the half of my goods I give to the poor, and if I have defrauded anyone of anything, I restore it fourfold."*
>
> *Luke 19:8–9*

Case Study: The Good Samaritan and the Reordering of Neighbor

A priest and Levite avoid costly compassion; a Samaritan interrupts his journey, spends his resources, and guarantees continued care. Kingdom ethics moves beyond obligation to sacrificial mercy, refusing to let ethnic, religious, or social boundaries limit love.

> *"Which of these three, do you think, proved to be a neighbor…? He said, 'The one who showed him mercy.' And Jesus said to him, 'You go, and do likewise.'"*
>
> *Luke 10:36–37*

Case Study: The Early Church—Equity and Order

Believers share possessions so none lack. When Greek-speaking widows are neglected, the apostles establish deacons to ensure fairness. Kingdom justice balances generosity with governance, spiritual power with administrative equity, protecting unity through a transparent process.

> *"And the twelve summoned the full number of the disciples and said… 'pick out from among you seven men of good repute… whom we will appoint to this duty.'*
>
> *Acts 6:2–3*

Case Study: Philemon, Onesimus, and Reconciling Power

Paul appeals for a runaway slave not merely as property but as a brother, asking Philemon to receive him as he would receive Paul. Kingdom justice interrupts social hierarchies, reinterprets identity in Christ, and calls those with authority to leverage it for reconciliation.

> *"For perhaps this is why he was parted from you for a while, that you might have him back forever, no longer as a bondservant but more than a bondservant, as a beloved brother."*
>
> *Philemon 15–16*

Domains of Ethical Practice: Personal, Communal, Vocational, Institutional

Personal holiness is the seedbed of public justice. We discipline appetites, tell the truth, keep covenant in marriage, steward money without greed, and refuse vengeance. We cultivate speech that blesses and confronts without slander. We confess quickly and forgive genuinely, rejecting the bitterness that fuels cycles of harm.

> *"Be kind to one another, tenderhearted, forgiving one another, as God in Christ forgave you."*
>
> *Ephesians 4:32*

Family and community become training grounds for justice. We honor parents and care for elders; we protect children and tell the truth across generations; we practice hospitality toward the marginalized and break bread with the lonely. Community disciplines that are redemptive, not punitive, guard unity and health.

> *"Let love be genuine. Abhor what is evil; hold fast to what is good."*
>
> *Romans 12:9*

Marketplace ethics display the Kingdom in contracts, wages, and truth in advertising. We pay laborers promptly, refuse bribery and kickbacks, and keep accurate books. We design products and policies that do not harm. We treat competitors with dignity and customers with honesty. Profit is stewarded, not worshiped.

> *"You shall not oppress your neighbor or rob him. The wages of a hired worker shall not remain with you all night until the morning."*
>
> *Leviticus 19:13*

Leadership ethics steward power as service. Authority is exercised without partiality; discipline is fair and proportionate; credit is shared and blame is owned. Leaders cultivate cultures where the weak are safe and the strong are accountable. Decisions are transparent, and corrections are public when harm was public.

> *"When one rules justly over men, ruling in the fear of God, he dawns on them like the morning light."*
>
> *2 Samuel 23:3–4*

Church governance embodies reconciliation and truth. We practice Matthew 18 processes with humility, protect the vulnerable, restore the repentant, and guard the table of the Lord with integrity. Offerings are handled with accountability; benevolence is administered with equity; teaching refuses favoritism and flattery.

> *"If your brother sins against you, go and tell him his fault, between you and him alone… if he listens to you, you have gained your brother."*
>
> *Matthew 18:15*

Public witness includes civic engagement without idolatry. We advocate for policies that protect life, dignity, and equity; we refuse to baptize partisanship as righteousness. We pray for rulers, speak truth to power, and embody alternative community that shows another way.

> *"Seek the welfare of the city where I have sent you into exile, and pray to the Lord on its behalf."*
>
> *Jeremiah 29:7*

Ethics in the Digital Age

Digital spaces require ancient virtues. We resist deception, outrage-for-profit, and the mob. We refuse voyeurism and exploitation. We verify before sharing, honor privacy, and repent publicly when we have harmed publicly. The screen does not suspend the command to love our neighbor.

> *"Whatever is true, whatever is honorable, whatever is just… think about these things."*
>
> *Philippians 4:8*

Justice, Mercy, and Humility Held Together

Justice without mercy becomes cruelty; mercy without justice becomes enablement; zeal without humility becomes self-righteousness. Kingdom ethics braids these strands in cruciform love. We remember that we, too, were strangers and sinners shown mercy. We correct with tears, not triumphalism; we serve from grace, not grievance.

> *"I desire mercy, and not sacrifice."*
>
> *Hosea 6:6*

Practices That Form a Just People

Daily examen and confession keep hearts tender. Fasting subdues appetites that distort judgment. Sabbath interrupts productivity and idolatry, and levels communities in rest. Shared tables train hospitality. Covenants and codes of conduct clarify expectations. Transparent financial systems, third-party audits, and open reporting protect integrity. Restitution plans accompany repentance. Peacemaking teams mediate conflicts. Mentoring multiplies ethical imagination. Vows for leaders anchor power to service. These practices are not legalism; they are trellises where Kingdom life can grow sturdy and sweet.

> *"By this all people will know that you are my disciples, if you have love for one another."*
>
> *John 13:35*

Warnings and Counterfeits

Beware of performative righteousness that acts just to be seen. Beware of selective outrage that denounces distant sins while excusing convenient ones. Beware of legalism that replaces the Spirit's power with human control. Beware of syncretism that baptizes cultural idols—greed, tribalism, celebrity, and domination—in religious language. Beware of exhaustion that mistakes busyness for obedience; justice flows from abiding in the King.

> *"I am the vine; you are the branches... apart from me you can do nothing."*
>
> *John 15:5*

Hope and the Future of Justice

Our labor is not in vain because the King will judge in righteousness and restore all things. New creation is not a private heaven but a renewed world where righteousness dwells. Every honest ledger, reconciled relationship, protected child, fair wage, and healed community anticipates that day. We practice now what will fill the earth then.

> *"But according to his promise we are waiting for new heavens and a new earth in which righteousness dwells."*
>
> *2 Peter 3:13*

> *"Behold, I am making all things new."*
>
> *Revelation 21:5*

Conclusion: The Testimony of a Just People

The Kingdom advances through a people whose ethics and justice bear the weight of the King's glory. We become salt that preserves against decay, light that exposes and heals, leaven that quietly transforms. In a culture discipled by appetite and power, our holy love and just deeds proclaim another government. Let our speech be truthful, our scales fair, our tables open, our leadership clean, our worship honest, and our repentance repair the harm. In all things may the character of the King be seen.

> *"Let your light shine before others, so that they may see your good works and give glory to your Father who is in heaven."*
>
> *Matthew 5:16*

Glossary of Key Terms

- ✔ Tsedeq (צֶדֶק): Righteousness; right alignment with God's ways expressed as ethical integrity and fairness.
- Mishpat (מִשְׁפָּט): Justice; right judgment and equitable order in community, including protection for the vulnerable.
- Tzedaqah (צְדָקָה): Righteous giving; generosity as a just obligation rooted in covenant faithfulness.
- Chesed (חֶסֶד): Covenant love; steadfast mercy and loyal kindness that sustains relationships beyond contract.
- Emet (אֱמֶת): Truth, reliability; that which is firm and faithful, the foundation of trustworthy speech and action.
- Emunah (אֱמוּנָה): Faith/faithfulness; steadfast reliability toward God and neighbor, often expressed in covenant loyalty.
- Shalom (שָׁלוֹם): Wholeness, peace, flourishing; right relationships with God, others, self, and creation.

CHAPTER 11

Legacy and Succession: Stewarding Kingdom Influence Across Generations

Introduction: The Kingdom Beyond a Lifetime

The Kingdom of God is eternal, yet our time on earth is limited. Every life carries a season of calling, responsibility, and assignment, but no life carries the entire Kingdom mandate. What we receive, we must also prepare to release. Legacy is not a memorial of our own greatness, but the enduring witness of God's reign carried forward through the lives of others. Succession is the deliberate stewardship of that witness so that what began in one generation does not perish with it, but multiplies across generations until the return of the King.

The God we serve is identified through His generational faithfulness—the God of Abraham, the God of Isaac, the God of Jacob. He is not the God of one leader only, nor the God of a single moment. He is the God who establishes His promises in such a way that children, grandchildren, and entire nations inherit them. His covenant intention was never to end with Abraham's obedience, but to perpetuate blessing to all the families of the earth. So it is with us: what we hold today is never ours alone. It is entrusted to us for the sake of those who come after us.

> *"Know therefore that the Lord your God is God, the faithful God who keeps covenant and steadfast love with those who love him and keep his commandments, to a thousand generations."*
>
> Deuteronomy 7:9

Legacy, then, is not only what we leave behind, but what we build into others while we are still present. Succession is not a transaction at the moment of death, but a posture of leadership that trains, empowers, and entrusts others while we still labor alongside them. To live Kingdom-minded is to live beyond our own lifetime.

The Weight of Legacy in Kingdom History

The record of Scripture bears witness to the necessity of legacy and succession. Abraham did not see the fullness of the promise but passed the covenant to Isaac. Isaac carried it to Jacob. Jacob spoke blessings over twelve sons, knowing that from them would rise a nation destined for covenant witness. Moses brought Israel to the edge of Canaan, but it was Joshua who led them in. David prepared materials for the temple, but Solomon was chosen to build it. Each generation completed part of the story, faithfully handing what they could not finish into the hands of the next.

Where this pattern was broken, decline followed. After the generation of Joshua passed, Judges records a devastating reality: there arose another generation who did not know the Lord or the works He had done for Israel. When fathers failed to tell their sons, and mothers neglected to impress the ways of God upon their daughters, memory was lost, covenant was neglected, and the people drifted into idolatry.

The victories of yesterday became meaningless when they were not carried forward into the discipline of today.

The Danger of Self-Centered Leadership

Leaders who clutch their influence too tightly, who seek to preserve their own name rather than empower successors, will inevitably see their work collapse once their hand is removed. The temptation of pride is to believe that we are indispensable, that nothing will stand unless we stand at its center. But Kingdom leadership is never about one personality. It is about covenant faithfulness that continues whether or not our names are remembered.

> *"Now these are the last words of David: The oracle of David, the son of Jesse, the oracle of the man who was raised on high… The Spirit of the Lord speaks by me, his word is on my tongue. The God of Israel has spoken; the Rock of Israel has said to me: When one rules justly over men, ruling in the fear of God, he dawns on them like the morning light."*
>
> *2 Samuel 23:1–4*

The strength of a leader is measured not only in victories won but in successors prepared. If our churches, ministries, businesses, or families collapse when we step aside, then we have failed to build a legacy. Succession is not an afterthought—it is a primary responsibility of stewardship

Succession as Covenant Continuity

Covenant continuity requires intentionality. Israel was commanded to teach the ways of God diligently to their children, speaking of them when they sat in their houses, when they walked by the way, when they lay down, and when they rose. This rhythm of daily transmission ensured that the next generation would not merely hear the Law as history but embody it as identity.

> *"You shall teach them diligently to your children, and shall talk of them when you sit in your house, and when you walk by the way, and when you lie down, and when you rise."*
>
> *Deuteronomy 6:7*

Succession in the Kingdom is not passive. It does not happen by accident. It must be cultivated through teaching, mentoring, modeling, and entrusting. Legacy is not secured by titles or inheritance alone, but by the impartation of values, convictions, and faith that anchor successors to the King Himself.

Case Study: Moses and Joshua

Moses spent years preparing Joshua before ever handing him the mantle. Joshua observed Moses interceding on the mountain, leading in battle, and judging the people. When Moses laid hands on Joshua, the act was not sudden or symbolic only—it was the public affirmation of what had already been cultivated privately. The people could trust Joshua because they had seen him walk faithfully under Moses. Succession succeeds when it is visible, gradual, and rooted in a relationship.

Case Study: Elijah and Elisha

Elijah's prophetic ministry culminated in the training of Elisha, who received a double portion of his spirit. Elisha's faithfulness to follow, to serve, and to persist ensured that the prophetic witness in Israel did not die with Elijah. This succession teaches us that true legacy is not threatened by successors who surpass us. On the contrary, it is strengthened by them. To leave a legacy in the Kingdom is to rejoice when those we have trained accomplish more than we did.

Case Study: Paul and Timothy

The apostle Paul poured himself into Timothy as a son in the faith. He entrusted him with teaching, correction, and pastoral oversight, instructing him to guard the deposit of truth. Paul knew his race was ending, but he also knew the Gospel would not end with him. Legacy was secured because truth was not bound to Paul's body, but entrusted to Timothy's spirit. Kingdom succession requires that we deposit truth into faithful people who will teach others also.

> *"What you have heard from me in the presence of many witnesses entrust to faithful men who will be able to teach others also."*
>
> *2 Timothy 2:2*

Stewarding Influence Beyond Personality

In every generation, leaders must distinguish between Kingdom influence and personal influence. Kingdom influence is rooted in

Christ, unshakable and transferable. Personal influence is bound to charisma, reputation, and human ability. If our ministries are built only on personal influence, they will fade when we do. If they are grounded in Kingdom influence, they will endure, for the Spirit of God works not through one vessel only, but through every vessel yielded to Him.

Legacy requires that we invest not only in tasks but in people. Strategies and systems may change with time, but people carry values, wisdom, and spiritual DNA across contexts. Succession is most secure when successors are shaped to think, discern, and act from Kingdom principles rather than merely mimic external behaviors.

Guarding Against Legacy Drift

Not all legacies remain pure. History is filled with examples of spiritual movements that began with fire but ended in compromise because successors did not maintain the same consecration as their forebears. Legacy must be guarded as well as given. To pass on values, we must also pass on disciplines—prayer, study, obedience, humility, and accountability. Without these, successors may inherit structures but lack the Spirit that birthed them.

This is why the apostolic letters often warn against false teaching, moral compromise, and cultural assimilation. Paul urged churches to hold fast to what had been taught, to cling to the traditions handed down, not out of rigidity but out of recognition that drift is easy and correction is costly. Legacy without vigilance becomes heritage without power.

The Role of Family in Legacy

Family is the first and primary sphere of succession. Before there are institutions, there are households. Abraham was chosen because he would command his children and his household after him to keep the way of the Lord. Parents who neglect discipleship in the home cannot expect their ministries or communities to endure. The Kingdom is secured first in the dinner table conversation, the evening prayer, and the example of faith lived before children's eyes.

> *"For I have chosen him, that he may command his children and his household after him to keep the way of the Lord by doing righteousness and justice, so that the Lord may bring to Abraham what he has promised him."*
>
> *Genesis 18:19*

Family succession is not limited to the bloodline. In the Kingdom, spiritual sons and daughters carry a legacy alongside biological heirs. Timothy was not Paul's son by blood, but by faith. Elisha was not Elijah's child, but he bore his prophetic inheritance. The Kingdom enlarges the family to include all who walk in covenant loyalty.

Succession and Transformation

True succession does not merely preserve; it transforms. Each generation must adapt the unchanging truth of God's Word to the new challenges of its time. A legacy that only repeats without renewing risks becoming a rigid tradition. Legacy that renews without remembering risks drifting from its foundation. Succession requires balance: faithfulness to what was given, and courage to apply it freshly.

This means that leaders must teach not only content but also how to discern. To pass on principles without training discernment is to raise successors who repeat formulas but cannot face new challenges. The Spirit, who guided us, must be the same Spirit guiding them. Legacy is not control but release, trusting that the same God who was faithful in our day will be faithful in theirs.

The Eternal Perspective of Legacy

Legacy in the Kingdom is not ultimately measured by earthly institutions or human remembrance. It is measured by the testimony of heaven. Some of the most faithful witnesses are unknown by name but remembered by God. Hebrews 11 records those who endured by faith, many of whom did not receive the fullness of what was promised, but their witness secured a better resurrection. Succession reminds us that our labor is not in vain, for it participates in an eternal Kingdom that cannot be shaken.

> *"Therefore, since we are surrounded by so great a cloud of witnesses, let us also lay aside every weight... and let us run with endurance the race that is set before us."*
>
> *Hebrews 12:1*

Conclusion: Building for a Thousand Generations

Every leader must ask: what am I building that will outlast me? What values, convictions, and disciplines am I depositing into the lives of others? Who is being prepared to carry forward what I cannot complete? Legacy is not an option—it is the inevitable outcome of every life. The only question is whether it will testify of the King or of ourselves.

To steward Kingdom influence is to remember that we are part of a story much larger than our own. We are custodians of a trust that belongs to Christ, builders of foundations others will stand upon, sowers of seed whose harvest we may never see. Our joy is not in finishing everything ourselves, but in knowing that the Kingdom will continue until the day when Christ returns and crowns the faithfulness of every generation.

Glossary of Key Terms

- Klēronomia (κληρονομία): Inheritance; spiritual trust and legacy passed on through generations.
- Diadokhē (διαδοχή): Succession; the orderly continuation of responsibility and leadership.
- Oikonomia (οἰκονομία): Stewardship; the management of resources and influence on behalf of the King.
- Martyria (μαρτυρία): Witness; the testimony carried forward through faithful lives.
- Pais (παῖς): Child, son or daughter; used for both natural children and disciples as heirs of legacy.
- Zakar (זָכַר): To remember; the act of recalling and transmitting covenant truth across generations.
- Nahal (נָחַל): To inherit; to receive as a possession or trust from one's forebears.
- Ben (בֵּן): Son; representative heir, whether biological or spiritual, who continues the family or covenant line

CHAPTER 12

All Things New: Toward the Consummation of the Kingdom

Introduction: The Eternal Horizon That Shapes Our Kingdom Journey

The life of the Kingdom is always lived with eyes fixed on an eternal horizon. The Scriptures remind us that the present form of this world is passing away, but the Kingdom is moving toward its consummation. This horizon is not a fading point in the distance; it is the reality that gives shape, meaning, and urgency to how we live today. Our obedience is not casual, our ethics not optional, our pursuit of justice not temporary, because each of these is anchored in the certainty that the King will return and make all things new. To live without this horizon is to live shortsighted, weighed down by the concerns of the moment. To live with it is to endure suffering with hope, to resist compromise with courage, and to walk in faith with assurance.

"Behold, I am making all things new."

The Consummation of the Kingdom

The Kingdom of God exists in the tension of the "already" and the "not yet." Through the death and resurrection of Christ, the Kingdom has already broken into history. We have received the Spirit as the down payment of our inheritance, and we taste the powers of the age to come. Yet we are still waiting for the fullness of the promise, for the day when death will be no more and the creation itself will be set free from corruption.

The Hebrew word chadash (חָדָשׁ) means new—not simply in the sense of recent, but renewed, restored, made fresh. The Greek kainos (καινός) carries this same sense of a newness that is different in kind, not just in time. The Consummation of the Kingdom is not the annihilation of the old but the transformation into the new. Creation will not be discarded like a worn-out garment, but remade into the fullness God intended from the beginning.

> *"For behold, I create new heavens and a new earth, and the former things shall not be remembered or come into mind."*
>
> *Isaiah 65:17*

This promise shapes the believer's vision of life. We do not labor in vain, for every righteous act, every faithful witness, and every sacrificial deed points toward the renewal of all things. Even the smallest acts of obedience are seeds planted in a soil that God Himself will one day cause to flourish in His eternal Kingdom.

Case Study: Noah and the Flood

The story of Noah is not only about judgment but also about renewal. The earth, corrupted by violence, was purged by the waters of the flood so that creation could begin again. Noah becomes a type of Christ, a righteous man who builds an ark of salvation. Yet the new world that emerges still carries the stain of sin, pointing us toward the need for a greater renewal than water alone can bring. The flood foreshadows the final renewal, when heaven and earth will be purged not by water but by fire, and creation will be fully restored under the reign of Christ.

> *"By the same word the heavens and earth that now exist are stored up for fire, being kept until the day of judgment and destruction of the ungodly."*
>
> 2 Peter 3:7

Like Noah, Kingdom leaders today are called to prepare communities that preserve righteousness amidst corruption. Just as Noah built an ark in obedience to a word others mocked, so we build Kingdom life today in ways the world may not understand. Our faithfulness prepares a testimony that points to the coming renewal.

The Eternal Horizon as Daily Motivation

The eternal horizon is not designed to detach us from daily life but to intensify our engagement. Paul calls the sufferings of this present time "light" when weighed against the eternal glory awaiting us. This does not minimize pain; it magnifies hope. When believers endure persecution, when leaders stand firm under cultural pressure, when families remain faithful despite hardship, it is because their eyes are set beyond the temporary.

The Greek word eschatos (ἔσχατος) means "last" or "final." From it we derive eschatology—the study of last things. Yet biblical eschatology is not speculation about dates or events; it is the posture of faith that lives in readiness. The last things shape the present things. To see the end is to know how to live now.

> *"For this light momentary affliction is preparing for us an eternal weight of glory beyond all comparison."*
>
> 2 Corinthians 4:17

Guarding the Boundaries of Kingdom Life

Until the Consummation, we live in a contested space. The Kingdom advances, but so does opposition. To live faithfully requires that we guard the boundaries of Kingdom life with vigilance. The Bride of Christ must be prepared without spot or wrinkle, preserved in holiness until the day of her Bridegroom's return.

Case Study: Nehemiah's Wall

When Nehemiah rebuilt Jerusalem's wall, it was not merely a political project but a spiritual one. The wall symbolized protection, identity, and separation from what defiled. In the same way, the people of God today must rebuild the walls of holiness and truth, even while living amidst ridicule and attack. Just as Nehemiah refused distraction and compromise, so must we resist the pressures of assimilation until the Consummation.

"I am doing a great work and I cannot come down."

Nehemiah 6:3

Guarding boundaries is not about exclusion but preservation. We guard the sacredness of worship, the integrity of teaching, the purity of leadership, and the witness of love. In an age where compromise is celebrated as tolerance, the Church must be clear: the eternal horizon belongs to a holy people.

Anticipation as Active Readiness

Jesus told parables of servants awaiting their master's return. Some were found faithful, stewarding resources and caring for fellow servants. Others grew careless, abusing authority, living as though the master would never come. The difference between them was not knowledge of the master's timing but readiness in the master's absence.

The Greek word parousia (παρουσία) means "coming" or "presence." To live in light of the parousia is to live as though the King's return could be at any moment. Anticipation reshapes priorities. We do not cling to possessions as though they are eternal, nor do we waste opportunities as though they are meaningless. Every moment becomes sacred because it is lived in view of His appearing.

The Renewal of Creation

Creation itself longs for renewal. Paul describes the world as groaning in labor pains, awaiting the revelation of the sons of God. This imagery tells us that history is not moving toward destruction but toward birth. The pains of this age are not meaningless—they are contractions pointing toward a new creation.

The Greek word apokatastasis (ἀποκατάστασις) means restoration, the bringing back of what was lost to its intended state. The Consummation is God's apokatastasis: the return of creation to its original harmony under the Lordship of Christ.

> *"For the creation waits with eager longing for the revealing of the sons of God."*
>
> *Romans 8:19*

This renewal means that our stewardship of creation now is Kingdom work. When we cultivate the land responsibly, when we protect life, when we steward resources with integrity, we testify to the reality that the earth is the Lord's and will be renewed under His reign.

The Consummation and Justice

Justice delayed is not justice denied in the Kingdom. The eternal horizon assures us that every injustice will one day be addressed. Leaders who labor for justice in the present do so not in vain but in hope. They may not see all wrongs righted in their lifetime, but they know that the Judge of all the earth will do right.

Case Study: John on Patmos

Exiled for his testimony, John received the vision of Revelation. From a place of suffering, he was given sight of the new Jerusalem descending from heaven. His personal exile did not silence his witness; it magnified it. Likewise, believers today who endure exile—whether social, cultural, or political—must lift their eyes to the eternal city. Our present marginalization is temporary; our eternal citizenship is secure.

"He will wipe away every tear from their eyes, and death shall be no more."

Revelation 21:4

Living in Anticipation Today

The eternal horizon shapes how we lead, how we govern, and how we live as families. Leaders guided by eternity resist corruption because they know their accountability is not to men alone but to Christ. Families teach children values that will outlast trends. Communities organize themselves not around temporary gain but around eternal truth.

Modern parallels abound. In an age where climate crisis threatens creation, the promise of renewal calls us to steward responsibly rather than exploit recklessly. In a society fractured by division, the vision of a united Bride calls us to labor for reconciliation now. In a digital culture addicted to distraction, the call to readiness challenges us to live alert, watchful, and faithful.

Conclusion: All Things New

The Consummation is not only the end of the old but the beginning of the eternal. The King will return, creation will be renewed, and the people of God will dwell in the presence of the Lamb forever. This vision is not meant to inspire speculation but transformation. We live differently because we see differently. Our labor is not wasted, our witness not forgotten, our faith not futile. We belong to a Kingdom that cannot be shaken, and we await a day when He will make all things new.

> *"According to his promise we are waiting for new heavens and a new earth in which righteousness dwells."*
>
> *2 Peter 3:13*

Glossary of Key Terms

- Chadash (חָדָשׁ): New; renewed, restored, fresh.
- Kainos (καινός): New in quality; different in kind, not merely recent.
- Eschatos (ἔσχατος): Last, final; from which eschatology derives.
- Parousia (παρουσία): Coming, presence; the return of Christ.
- Apokatastasis (ἀποκατάστασις): Restoration, returning creation to intended harmony.
- Shalom (שָׁלוֹם): Wholeness, peace, flourishing in renewed creation

CHAPTER 13

Kingdom Leadership and Authority: Walking in the King's Delegated Power

Introduction: Authority Anchored in the King

Every Kingdom leader must understand that authority does not originate in themselves. All authority belongs to God. Any authority we exercise is borrowed, delegated, and accountable. To forget this is to abuse leadership. To remember it is to walk in humility, strength, and faithfulness. The King is the source, and we are His stewards. Authority without anchoring in Him becomes tyranny. Authority rooted in Him becomes service that blesses, protects, and advances the Kingdom.

> *"For there is no authority except from God, and those that exist have been instituted by God."*
>
> *Romans 13:1*

Authority Defined in the Kingdom

In the Scriptures, authority is never abstract. The Hebrew word śar (שַׂר) describes rulers, officials, and commanders—those entrusted with oversight. The word shalit (שָׁלִיט) refers to one empowered to act, to govern, or to exercise control. In the Greek, exousia (ἐξουσία) describes delegated authority—the right to act on behalf of another. Authority in the Kingdom is not self-derived but given. It is the legal right and spiritual empowerment to represent the King.

When Jesus taught, people marveled because He spoke "as one having authority" and not as their scribes. His authority was not borrowed from tradition or dependent on human approval. It came from His identity as the Son of God. When He healed the sick and cast out demons, the powers of darkness recognized His authority and obeyed. When He forgave sins, He revealed the highest authority of all—the authority to reconcile humanity to the Father.

> *"All authority in heaven and on earth has been given to me. Go therefore and make disciples of all nations."*
>
> *Matthew 28:18–19*

Authority Delegated to Leaders

From the beginning, God designed humanity to share in His authority. Adam and Eve were commissioned to exercise dominion over creation, not to exploit it but to steward it as representatives of the Creator. Though sin corrupted this vocation, God's design was never revoked. Through Christ, the mandate is restored and reoriented. Kingdom leadership means exercising God's authority in God's way, for God's purposes.

Jesus entrusted authority to His disciples. He sent the Twelve with authority over unclean spirits and power to heal. He later commissioned the seventy-two, who returned rejoicing that even demons were subject to them in His name. The Greek word dynamis (δύναμις) describes power, ability, and capacity; exousia clarifies that this power is lawful because it is authorized. Leaders today walk in that same delegated authority—not in their own name, but in His.

Case Study: The Roman Centurion

A centurion approached Jesus on behalf of his paralyzed servant. He declared that he was not worthy for Jesus to enter his house, but believed that a word from Him was enough. The centurion explained his understanding: "For I too am a man under authority, with soldiers under me." He recognized that true authority flows from being under authority. His faith amazed Jesus because it grasped the essence of Kingdom leadership—submission precedes command.

This principle holds today. Leaders who refuse accountability cannot wield true authority. Those who will not be under authority should not be trusted with authority. In the Kingdom, power flows through alignment. The greater the submission, the clearer the authority.

Authority as Service, Not Domination

Jesus redefined leadership authority by linking it to service. In the world, rulers lord authority over others. In the Kingdom, the greatest is the one who serves. Authority is not a license to control but empowerment to lift, to guard, and to guide. The authority of the shepherd is seen in his care for the flock, not in the display of his power.

> *"The greatest among you shall be your servant."*
>
> *Matthew 23:11*

Case Study: Moses and Shared Authority

Moses, overwhelmed by the burden of leading Israel, cried out for relief. God instructed him to gather seventy elders, and He placed some of the Spirit that was on Moses upon them. Authority was shared so that the people could be shepherded with justice. This distribution of authority prevented collapse and ensured continuity. Leaders today must learn that authority is multiplied, not diminished, when it is shared with faithful stewards.

Case Study: Paul's Apostolic Authority

Paul constantly defended his apostleship not to secure personal recognition but to protect the Gospel. His authority was rooted in his encounter with the risen Christ and confirmed by the fruit of his ministry. Yet Paul consistently reminded churches that his authority was for building them up, not tearing them down. Kingdom authority is protective, constructive, and restorative.

> *"For even if I boast a little too much of our authority, which the Lord gave for building you up and not for destroying you, I will not be ashamed."*
>
> 2 Corinthians 10:8

Authority and Spiritual Warfare

Kingdom authority also extends into the spiritual realm. Leaders are not only administrators but also guardians of the flock against wolves and principalities. The Church is called to bind and loose, to resist the devil, to stand in the armor of God. Authority here is not about shouting louder but standing firmer—knowing our position in Christ.

> *"Behold, I have given you authority to tread on serpents and scorpions, and over all the power of the enemy, and nothing shall hurt you."*
>
> Luke 10:19

Authority Misused and Abused

History testifies to the dangers of authority divorced from accountability. Kings of Israel fell when they used authority for personal gain rather than covenant faithfulness. Church leaders throughout history have erred when authority became self-serving. Authority without humility becomes domination; authority without love becomes cruelty; authority without accountability becomes corruption. Leaders must constantly return to the model of Christ, who washed feet even as He held all authority.

Guarding the Boundaries of Authority

Authority in the Kingdom is not unlimited. It has boundaries set by the King. Leaders may not act outside of His Word or contrary to His Spirit. Authority exercised for personal advancement is rebellion. Authority exercised in obedience is worship. Leaders must discern where their authority begins and ends, lest they trespass into what belongs to God alone.

Modern Application: Authority in Today's World

In a world suspicious of authority because of its abuses, Kingdom leaders must embody a different model. In the home, parents exercise authority not as tyrants but as nurturers. In the church, pastors lead not as CEOs but as shepherds. In organizations, Christian leaders must balance strength with humility, justice with mercy. In civic life, believers entrusted with authority must remember they answer first to the King of kings.

Modern parallels show the crisis of authority today: political leaders manipulating truth, corporate executives exploiting workers, even spiritual leaders using influence for personal empire. Against this backdrop, Kingdom leadership must shine as a contrast—transparent, accountable, sacrificial. Authority rooted in the King will bring restoration where worldly authority has brought harm.

Conclusion: Authority Anchored in the King

All Kingdom authority is anchored in Christ. He holds all authority in heaven and on earth. We walk in delegated power, not our own. Our authority is measured by our alignment with Him, our submission to His Word, and our faithfulness to His people. Leaders who grasp this walk with confidence but also with trembling. We are not owners of power but stewards of the King's trust. Our authority must always point back to Him, until the day when He returns and every crown is cast at His feet.

"To him be dominion forever and ever. Amen."

1 Peter 5:11

Glossary of Key Terms

- Śar (שַׂר): Ruler, official, commander entrusted with oversight.
- Shalit (שַׁלִּיט): One empowered to govern or exercise control.
- Exousia (ἐξουσία): Delegated authority, lawful right to act on another's behalf.
- Dynamis (δύναμις): Power, ability, supernatural capacity.
- Kratos (κράτος): Dominion, strength, ruling might.
- Diakonia (διακονία): Service, ministry; the true exercise of authority as servanthood.

CHAPTER 14

The Eternal Journey: Living in the Fullness of the Kingdom

Introduction: The Lifelong Pilgrimage Toward Kingdom Maturity

To belong to the Kingdom of God is to be set upon a journey that does not end in this lifetime. The call of the King is not only to salvation but to pilgrimage—a lifelong pursuit of maturity, faithfulness, and transformation. The Kingdom is not static; it is living, advancing, and ever drawing us deeper into the fullness of God's design. Each day of obedience, each trial endured, each lesson embraced becomes a step along this eternal road. We are pilgrims walking toward a city whose architect and builder is God.

"For here we have no lasting city, but we seek the city that is to come."

Hebrews 13:14

The Eternal Nature of the Journey

From Genesis to Revelation, the people of God are presented as sojourners. Abraham was called to leave his homeland and journey toward a promise he would not see fulfilled in his lifetime. Israel wandered through the wilderness on their way to Canaan. The exiles of Judah wept by the rivers of Babylon while hoping for restoration. The disciples followed Christ, not knowing where the road would lead. Each of these stories testifies that the Kingdom life is not about standing still but about pressing forward.

The Hebrew word halak (הָלַךְ) means "to walk" or "to journey." It conveys movement, progress, and direction. To walk with God is to refuse stagnation. It is to keep moving even when the way is unclear, trusting that the One who called is faithful. The Greek word hodos (ὁδός) means "way" or "path," used repeatedly in the New Testament to describe the life of discipleship. Followers of Jesus were even called "The Way," emphasizing that Christianity is not a static religion but a dynamic journey with Christ.

> "Blessed are those whose strength is in you, in whose heart are the highways to Zion."
>
> Psalm 84:5

Kingdom Maturity as Pilgrimage

The journey of the Kingdom is not measured in years but in growth. Maturity is the true mark of progress. The Hebrew word tamim (תָּמִים) describes being blameless, whole, or complete. The Greek teleios (τέλειος) carries the sense of being mature, fully grown, complete in character. Kingdom maturity is not perfection in the sense of flawlessness, but wholeness in the sense of alignment with God's purpose.

Case Study: Abraham's Pilgrimage

Abraham's life illustrates Kingdom pilgrimage. Called from Ur, he wandered as a stranger in Canaan, living in tents though promised the land. His journey was marked by altars, where he built places of worship as milestones of faith. He stumbled at times—fearing for his life, doubting God's timing—but he pressed on. His legacy is summed up not by perfection but by faith that endured the journey. Abraham teaches us that pilgrimage is not without failure, but it is defined by persistence.

> *"By faith Abraham obeyed when he was called to go out to a place that he was to receive as an inheritance."*
>
> Hebrews 11:8

The Pilgrimage of Israel

Israel's forty years in the wilderness show that the journey can either produce maturity or expose unbelief. Though God provided manna, water, and guidance, many grumbled and resisted. Their pilgrimage became a mirror of the heart: some grew in faith, others fell in rebellion. For leaders today, the wilderness seasons test whether we trust God's provision or turn back to Egypt. Pilgrimage requires endurance and faith in God's direction, even when the way seems endless.

> *"Remember the whole way that the Lord your God has led you these forty years in the wilderness, that he might humble you, testing you to know what was in your heart."*
>
> Deuteronomy 8:2

The Apostolic Vision of Journey

Paul described his life as a race to be run, a prize to be obtained, a goal toward which he pressed. His language of pilgrimage was active and relentless. He did not claim to have arrived, but confessed that he strained forward. His letters remind us that maturity is not passive but pursued.

> *"I press on toward the goal for the prize of the upward call of God in Christ Jesus."*
>
> *Philippians 3:14*

Paul's use of teleios for maturity reminds us that the journey is not optional for Kingdom citizens. Immaturity is dangerous; it leaves the believer vulnerable to false teaching, tossed by waves of doctrine. Maturity, by contrast, equips us to discern truth, to lead faithfully, and to endure hardship.

The Eternal Dimension of Pilgrimage

Pilgrimage does not end with death. The book of Revelation describes the saints as those who follow the Lamb wherever He goes. The eternal Kingdom is not static repose but unending life, dynamic worship, and perpetual discovery of God's glory. The eternal journey is not a burden but a delight. Our present pilgrimage is preparation for that eternal fullness.

> *"They will see his face, and his name will be on their foreheads. And night will be no more."*
>
> Revelation 22:4–5

Guarding Maturity in a Distracted Age

Today, the danger of distraction is perhaps the greatest threat to Kingdom pilgrimage. Unlike Israel, who faced wilderness hunger, or the early church, who faced persecution, modern believers often face the subtle erosion of purpose through comfort, entertainment, and busyness. The eternal journey requires focus. Leaders must guard their communities from trivial pursuits that masquerade as purpose. We must teach believers to number their days, to redeem the time, to live as pilgrims and not settlers.

Modern Application: Pilgrimage in Our World

The image of pilgrimage speaks powerfully into our contemporary world. Families fractured by consumerism need to rediscover the discipline of walking together toward a common goal. Churches distracted by programs must return to the simplicity of following the Lamb. Leaders tempted to build monuments to themselves must remember they are only guides on a journey toward another City.

Case Study: John on Patmos

Exiled on an island, John could have seen his journey as ended. Yet it was in that place of isolation that he was caught up in the Spirit and given the vision of the eternal city. His pilgrimage continued, even in exile. This teaches us that no circumstance can halt the eternal journey of the Kingdom citizen. Whether in freedom or in exile, in prosperity or in scarcity, the journey goes on.

Conclusion: The Pilgrimage That Leads to Fullness

The eternal journey is not about wandering aimlessly but walking purposefully toward fullness in Christ. To live in the fullness of the Kingdom is to embrace maturity, to walk faithfully, to endure trials, and to keep pressing toward the eternal horizon. Our pilgrimage will one day culminate in the presence of the King, but until then, every step matters. We are not settlers in this world; we are pilgrims pressing on toward the fullness of the Kingdom.

> *"For we walk by faith, not by sight."*
>
> *2 Corinthians 5:7*

Glossary of Key Terms

- Halak (הָלַךְ): To walk, to journey; the way of life with God.
- Tamim (תָּמִים): Blameless, whole, mature, complete in purpose.
- Teleios (τέλειος): Mature, complete, fully grown in Christ.
- Hodos (ὁδός): The way, the path; used of discipleship and pilgrimage.
- Parepidēmos (παρεπίδημος): Sojourner, pilgrim, stranger in a foreign land

CHAPTER 15

The Eternal Inheritance: Receiving What Cannot Be Shaken

Introduction: Anchored in Promise, Living for What Lasts

Every generation seeks to leave something behind, whether in wealth, reputation, or memory. Yet all earthly inheritances fade, corrode, or fracture in the hands of heirs. Kingdom inheritance, however, is eternal, unshakable, and reserved for those who belong to Christ. It is not limited to land or possessions but encompasses righteousness, life, glory, and the fullness of God's reign. To live as Kingdom citizens is to recognize that our truest inheritance is not of this world but of the world to come, and yet its power already shapes how we live today.

> *"Therefore let us be grateful for receiving a kingdom that cannot be shaken, and thus let us offer to God acceptable worship, with reverence and awe."*
>
> *Hebrews 12:28*

The Promise of Inheritance

The Hebrew word nahal (נָחַל) means "to inherit, to receive as a possession." Israel was promised an inheritance in the land of Canaan, a tangible testimony of God's covenant faithfulness. That inheritance was not earned but received — given by promise, sustained by obedience, and forfeited by rebellion. The land stood as a signpost pointing forward to a greater inheritance, one not bound to soil but to the eternal covenant of God.

The Greek klēronomia (κληρονομία) means "inheritance," a legal transfer of possession. Paul uses this term to describe what believers receive in Christ: forgiveness, the Spirit, eternal life, and glory. Unlike earthly inheritances that diminish with each division, Kingdom inheritance multiplies without depletion, given freely to every child of God.

> *"In him we have obtained an inheritance, having been predestined according to the purpose of him who works all things according to the counsel of his will."*
>
> *Ephesians 1:11*

Israel's Pattern and Our Promise

Israel's inheritance teaches us three truths. First, inheritance is rooted in promise. God told Abraham that his descendants would inherit the land, and that promise sustained generations. Second, inheritance requires obedience. While the land was given, possession depended on Israel's faithfulness. Third, inheritance can be forfeited. Through idolatry and injustice, Israel lost the fullness of what God intended, reminding us that inheritance is not to be presumed upon but stewarded.

These truths apply to Kingdom inheritance today. We are heirs not by merit but by promise. Yet the call remains to walk in obedience, for those who live contrary to the Spirit cannot inherit the Kingdom of God. And though our inheritance in Christ cannot be taken away, our experience of its fullness can be hindered by disobedience.

> *"Do you not know that the unrighteous will not inherit the kingdom of God? Do not be deceived…"*
>
> *1 Corinthians 6:9*

Case Study: The Prodigal and the Elder Son

Jesus' parable of the prodigal son reveals much about inheritance. The younger son demanded his share prematurely, squandering it in recklessness. The elder son, though outwardly faithful, failed to rejoice in his father's generosity. Both misunderstood inheritance. One saw it as possession for indulgence; the other as wages for labor. The father, however, revealed inheritance as a relationship: "Son, you are always with me, and all that is mine is yours."

Kingdom inheritance is not a prize we demand nor wages we earn. It is the Father's gift, rooted in relationship. To live as heirs is to live in the joy of sonship, not in striving or indulgence.

Co-Heirs with Christ

Christ is the firstborn heir, the true Israel, who fulfills the promise of inheritance. In Him, we are adopted as sons and daughters, made co-heirs of all that belongs to Him. This means we share in His sufferings as well as His glory. To be co-heirs is to participate in both the cross and the crown, in sacrifice and in exaltation.

> *"The Spirit himself bears witness with our spirit that we are children of God, and if children, then heirs—heirs of God and fellow heirs with Christ, provided we suffer with him in order that we may also be glorified with him."*
>
> *Romans 8:16–17*

Our inheritance is not freedom from hardship but participation in eternal glory. We are not heirs of comfort but of a Kingdom that endures beyond the shaking of nations.

Inheritance for Today

Though our inheritance is eternal, it has present implications. Believers live now as heirs, and that identity shapes our decisions, priorities, and endurance.

- ✔ Identity: Knowing we are heirs delivers us from striving. We are not orphans scrambling for scraps, but sons and daughters secure in the Father's promise.
- ✔ Holiness: Inheritance calls us to purity. Heirs live differently, preparing to steward what is holy.
- ✔ Generosity: Kingdom heirs are not possessive but open-handed, for our treasure is not depleted by giving.

✔ Hope: Inheritance gives us courage to endure trials, knowing that present suffering cannot compare to future glory.

> *"Blessed be the God and Father of our Lord Jesus Christ! According to his great mercy, he has caused us to be born again to a living hope… to an inheritance that is imperishable, undefiled, and unfading, kept in heaven for you."*
>
> *1 Peter 1:3–4*

Case Study: Broken Legacies Today

Many families today fracture over inheritance. Estates are contested, siblings are divided, legacies squandered. These conflicts expose the futility of earthly possessions. In contrast, Kingdom inheritance unites rather than divides, multiplies rather than diminishes, and endures rather than fades. In churches and ministries, leaders must model this reality, passing on not just property or titles but faith, wisdom, and integrity. Kingdom inheritance is not about keeping our names alive but about securing the witness of Christ across generations.

Inheriting What Cannot Be Shaken

Hebrews declares that we have received "a kingdom that cannot be shaken." Nations fall, economies collapse, empires fade, but the inheritance of the saints remains unshakable. This inheritance is not land but life, not wealth but glory, not legacy but eternity. It is the unbreakable covenant sealed in the blood of Christ.

To live as heirs of an unshakable Kingdom is to hold earthly possessions lightly, to endure trials with hope, and to build not on sand but on rock. It is to live in gratitude, worship, and reverence, knowing that what awaits us is beyond imagination.

Conclusion: Living as Heirs Now

Inheritance shapes how we live now. As heirs of God and co-heirs with Christ, we must:

- ✔ Live in gratitude, for all is a gift.
- ✔ Walk in obedience, for inheritance is holy.
- ✔ Endure suffering, for glory is coming.
- ✔ Pass on legacy, for the next generation must inherit faith.

To be Kingdomish is to live as heirs of what cannot be shaken, anchored in promise and living for what lasts.

Glossary of Key Terms

- Nahal (נָחַל) – To inherit, to receive possession. Root of Israel's inheritance in the land.
- Klēronomia (κληρονομία) – Inheritance; legal possession, often used for eternal inheritance in Christ.
- Sygklēronomos (συγκληρονόμος) – Co-heir; one who shares equally in inheritance, used of believers in Christ.
- Tamim (תָּמִים) – Whole, blameless; the character of one fit to steward inheritance.

CHAPTER 16

The King's People, The King's Reign

Introduction: Living as Citizens of the Unshakable Kingdom

The Kingdom of God does not end with theory, nor does it rest on the shoulders of isolated leaders. Its consummation is revealed through a people who live together under the reign of the King. The final vision of Scripture is not of individuals scattered across eternity but of a multitude gathered, redeemed, and transformed—a holy nation bearing the King's name. To be a Kingdom citizen is to belong to something larger than oneself, to embody together the reign of Christ in the world today while anticipating its eternal fullness.

> *"Therefore let us be grateful for receiving a kingdom that cannot be shaken, and thus let us offer to God acceptable worship, with reverence and awe."*
>
> Hebrews 12:28

The Nature of Kingdom Citizenship

The Greek word basileia (βασιλεία) describes the reign and rule of a king. The Kingdom is not merely a territory but the active authority of

God expressed through His people. Citizenship in this Kingdom is not achieved by birth into a nation or by membership in an institution. It is granted through new birth in Christ, sealed by the Spirit, and demonstrated by obedience.

The Hebrew word qahal (קָהָל) refers to the assembly or congregation of God's people, the gathered body called into covenant. In the New Testament, this becomes the ekklesia (ἐκκλησία), the called-out ones who live as the visible expression of Kingdom life in the world. Kingdom citizenship is not abstract; it is lived out in community, shaped by covenant, and marked by holiness.

> *"You are a chosen race, a royal priesthood, a holy nation, a people for his own possession."*
>
> 1 Peter 2:9

The King's People as a Witnessing Community

Throughout history, God's people have been His witnesses in the earth. Israel was called to be a light to the nations, displaying the wisdom and justice of God through their laws, festivals, and worship. The church, grafted into that covenant story, is likewise called to embody the reign of Christ in visible, tangible ways. Our unity, holiness, generosity, and justice are not just personal virtues—they are testimonies of the King's reign.

Case Study: Israel at Sinai

At Mount Sinai, Israel was constituted as a nation under God's direct rule. Their laws, feasts, and tabernacle worship were not cultural artifacts but covenantal markers of Kingdom identity. By living differently, they declared to surrounding nations that there is one true King. Their failure came when they sought to be like other nations, exchanging distinctiveness for assimilation. For today's church, the warning remains: we are called to embody a different order, not to mimic the systems of the world.

Case Study: The Early Church

The early church in Jerusalem lived as a Kingdom community. They shared possessions, devoted themselves to the apostles' teaching, broke bread together, and prayed with one accord. Their life of unity and generosity was so distinct that outsiders took notice. Even amidst persecution, their witness could not be silenced. This community, weak in worldly power but rich in Kingdom life, turned the world upside down.

> *"They devoted themselves to the apostles' teaching and the fellowship, to the breaking of bread and the prayers."*
>
> *Acts 2:42*

The Reign of the King in Every Sphere

The reign of Christ is not limited to religious spaces. It permeates every sphere of life—family, work, governance, culture. Kingdom citizens are called to display the King's justice in business, His mercy in relationships, His truth in education, His holiness in worship, His creativity in the arts. Wherever we live, the reign of the King must be visible.

This is what it means to pray, "Your kingdom come, your will be done, on earth as it is in heaven." It is not a passive hope but an active calling. When leaders govern with integrity, when families live in covenant faithfulness, when communities resist injustice and practice mercy, the reign of Christ breaks into the present age.

Guarding the Unity of the King's People

The greatest threat to the witness of the King's people is division. Jesus prayed that His disciples would be one so that the world would believe. Division distorts the witness of the Kingdom, suggesting that the King's power is insufficient to reconcile His people. Unity does not mean uniformity, but it requires humility, forgiveness, and covenant love.

Case Study: Paul and the Corinthian Church

The Corinthian church was rich in gifts but poor in unity. Paul admonished them for aligning themselves under different teachers, forgetting that they were one body under one Lord. He reminded them that love is the greatest gift, the foundation of all Kingdom life. For the church today, the lesson is clear: spiritual gifts without covenant love are noise; authority without unity is weakness.

> *"For in one Spirit we were all baptized into one body—Jews or Greeks, slaves or free—and all were made to drink of one Spirit."*
>
> *1 Corinthians 12:13*

The People Who Bear the King's Name

To carry the name of the King is to live in a way that reflects His character. The Hebrew word shem (שֵׁם), meaning name, signifies reputation and identity. God placed His name upon Israel as His covenant people. Today, Christ places His name upon the church. Our conduct either honors or dishonors that name. Kingdom citizenship is therefore a sacred trust: we bear the name of the King wherever we go.

> *"They will see his face, and his name will be on their foreheads."*
>
> *Revelation 22:4*

Modern Application: The King's People in Today's World

In a fractured and polarized world, the King's people are called to embody a unity that transcends tribe, nation, race, and ideology. In an age of corruption, they are to lead with integrity. In a culture obsessed with self, they are to live with sacrificial love. In a time of despair, they are to embody hope rooted in the eternal horizon. Our witness is not in programs or strategies alone, but in the way we live together as citizens of the Kingdom.

Case Study: Global Church Movements

Across the world today, movements of believers gather in homes, fields, schools, and public squares. Some meet under persecution, others in freedom. Yet what unites them is not culture, language, or denomination but allegiance to the King. Their witness reveals that the Kingdom is not bound to one nation or expression but is global, multiethnic, and eternal.

Conclusion: The King's People, The King's Reign

The Kingdom is not only about a coming age; it is about a present people. We are called to live now as citizens of the unshakable Kingdom, embodying together the reign of the King. Our unity, holiness, justice, and love declare to the world that the King has come and will come again. The story of Kingdomish does not end with theory but with calling. We are the King's people, entrusted with His reign, witnesses to His glory, and participants in His eternal plan. Let us walk worthy of that calling until the day when we stand together before the throne and hear the voice of the King declare, "Behold, I am making all things new."

Glossary of Key Terms

- Basileia (βασιλεία): Kingdom, reign, rule of a king.
- Qahal (קָהָל): Assembly, congregation; covenant people of God.
- Ekklesia (ἐκκλησία): Called-out ones, the gathered body of believers.
- Laos (λαός): People; used for God's covenant people.
- Shem (שֵׁם): Name, reputation, identity; to bear the name of the King.

EPILOGUE

The Unshakable Kingdom and the Call of Today

Every page of this journey has pressed us toward one truth: the Kingdom of God is not an abstract idea, nor a distant hope. It is the present reality of the King's reign breaking into our lives, demanding our obedience, shaping our character, and calling us to walk differently in the world. To be Kingdom citizens is to live as if the reign of Christ is already here—because it is. It is to anticipate the day when His reign will be seen in fullness and to live now as witnesses of that coming age.

We have seen that the Kingdom is ethical—it demands righteousness and justice. It is covenantal—it requires faithfulness across generations. It is eschatological—it points us toward the consummation when all things will be made new. It is communal—it forms us as a people, not as scattered individuals. It is spiritual—it equips us to stand in authority, to guard boundaries, to serve in humility. And it is eternal—it calls us to a pilgrimage that will not end with this age but will stretch into the fullness of God's glory forever.

The call before us is not to admire these truths but to embody them. We are summoned to be the King's people in the midst of a fractured age, to display His justice in unjust systems, His mercy in merciless cultures, His holiness in a compromised world, and His hope in an age of despair. The Kingdom is not a theory. It is life, it is power, it is truth embodied in us.

> *"Therefore, since we are surrounded by so great a cloud of witnesses, let us also lay aside every weight, and sin which clings so closely, and let us run with endurance the race that is set before us, looking to Jesus, the founder and perfecter of our faith."*
>
> *Hebrews 12:1–2*

This is our inheritance, our calling, and our responsibility. The King has entrusted His reign to us in this present age, not to build our own empires, but to display His glory. We are witnesses of His Kingdom until He comes. We are to live as salt and light, as leaven in the dough, as ambassadors of reconciliation, as sons and daughters who reflect the Father's heart.

The time is urgent. The world is groaning. The Bride must prepare herself. This is not a moment to retreat, nor a time to assimilate. It is the hour to rise as Kingdom citizens, walking in the fullness of what has been revealed, pressing toward maturity, and bearing witness until the day of consummation.

This is Kingdomish—the call to live all of life under the reign of the King. May we be found faithful, may we hand this legacy to generations yet unborn, and may we stand together on that day when the voice from the throne declares, "Behold, the dwelling place of God is with man." Until then, let us walk worthy of the calling we have received

RECOMMENDED READING

On the Kingdom of God

- George Eldon Ladd, The Gospel of the Kingdom
- Dallas Willard, The Divine Conspiracy
- N. T. Wright, How God Became King

On Covenant, Ethics, and Justice

- Christopher J. H. Wright, Old Testament Ethics for the People of God
- John Howard Yoder, The Politics of Jesus
- Miroslav Volf, Exclusion and Embrace

On Leadership and Formation

- Henri J. M. Nouwen, In the Name of Jesus
- W. Tozer, The Pursuit of God
- Richard J. Foster, Celebration of Discipline

On Identity and Inheritance

- Watchman Nee, The Normal Christian Life
- Derek Prince, Blessing or Curse
- J. I. Packer, Knowing God

On Spiritual Authority and the Church

- Watchman Nee, Spiritual Authority
- Edmund P. Clowney, The Church
- Eugene Peterson, The Pastor: A Memoir

ABOUT THE KINGDOM FORMATION SERIES

The Kingdom Formation Series is a three-volume journey into the truth, culture, and authority of the Kingdom of God.

The first book, Kingdomish, reclaims the original call of the believer by confronting compromise and clarifying what it means to live fully under the reign of Christ. It provides a prophetic foundation for Kingdom citizenship, ethics, justice, and leadership.

The second book, The King's Kings (forthcoming), will explore the believer's identity as both priest and ruler. It will trace the stages of calling, ordination, and commissioning, providing a framework for Kingdom leadership in every sphere.

The third book, Kingdom Proper (forthcoming), will complete the trilogy by guiding readers into the fullness of Kingdom maturity and eternal citizenship. It will examine the realities of building in unity, resisting dissonance, and preparing for the consummation of all things.

Together, these works form the Kingdom Formation Series—a pathway of transformation that equips leaders, disciples, and communities to embody the King's character and steward His legacy until He returns.

APPENDICES

Appendix A

The Ashlar Stone and Kingdom Building

The metaphor of the ashlar stone describes refinement, alignment, and preparation for Kingdom purpose. In ancient construction, an ashlar was a stone carefully cut in the quarry, shaped with precision so it could fit perfectly into a temple or palace. Unlike rough stones left unshaped, the ashlar bore the marks of intentional work. Kingdom citizens, too, are called to become ashlars—stones refined and prepared for the Master Builder's design.

> *"You yourselves like living stones are being built up as a spiritual house, to be a holy priesthood, to offer spiritual sacrifices acceptable to God through Jesus Christ."*
>
> *1 Peter 2:5*

The temple stones were shaped in hiddenness, far from the public eye, so that no sound of iron tools was heard at the site. This shows us that much of God's work in us takes place in unseen seasons. He chisels pride, fear, and selfishness from our lives so that we may bear weight without cracking. Discipline is not punishment but preparation.

> *"The house, when it was built, was with stone prepared at the quarry, so that neither hammer nor axe nor any tool of iron was heard in the house while it was being built."*
>
> 1 Kings 6:7

Solomon's temple was built with ashlars; the church is built with living stones. Discipleship is the shaping process, moving believers from rough stone to fitted stone. Conversion brings us out of the quarry, but formation prepares us for placement. Congregations that resist formation remain fragile; those that embrace refinement stand firm.

The ashlar life is marked by integrity, humility, and alignment. God does not place us into His Kingdom structure until He has made us fit for His purpose. To resist the process is to remain unformed. To embrace it is to become part of an eternal structure that will never collapse.

> *"Behold, I am laying in Zion a stone, a tested stone, a precious cornerstone, of a sure foundation: whoever believes will not be in haste."*
>
> Isaiah 28:1

Appendix B

Cognitive Dissonance and Kingdom Alignment

Cognitive dissonance is the inner tension that arises when belief and behavior do not align. In Kingdom life, it is the contradiction of professing loyalty to the King while living in compromise. This double-mindedness fractures our witness and drains our strength.

> *"The double-minded man is unstable in all his ways."*
>
> *James 1:8*

The Hebrew word lev (לֵב), meaning heart, speaks of the center of thought, will, and desire. When our heart is divided, dissonance emerges. The Greek word dipsychos (δίψυχος) means "double-souled." James warns that such instability renders one ineffective in faith.

Israel in the wilderness illustrates dissonance. They sang God's praise at the Red Sea yet longed for Egypt soon after. Their mouths confessed freedom but their hearts desired bondage. Likewise, Ananias and Sapphira presented themselves as fully surrendered while secretly withholding. Their duplicity provoked judgment because it fractured covenant integrity.

> *"You have not lied to man but to God."*
>
> *Acts 5:4*

Kingdom alignment means wholeness. The Hebrew tamim (תָּמִים) describes completeness and integrity. The Greek homologeō (ὁμολογέω) means to confess, to agree with God. Alignment dissolves dissonance by uniting word and deed, faith and practice.

> *"Teach me your way, O Lord, that I may walk in your truth; unite my heart to fear your name."*
>
> *Psalm 86:11*

To walk in alignment is to be whole. To remain in dissonance is to live fractured and unstable. The Spirit calls us to resolve dissonance by surrendering every thought, desire, and action to the reign of Christ.

Appendix C

Consolidated Glossary of Key Hebrew and Greek Terms

Hebrew Terms

- Eben (אֶבֶן) – Stone; symbol of witness, covenant, and formation.
- Tsedeq (צֶדֶק) – Righteousness; alignment with God's order.
- Mishpat (מִשְׁפָּט) – Justice; equity and fairness rooted in covenant.
- Chesed (חֶסֶד) – Steadfast love; covenant loyalty and mercy.
- Shalom (שָׁלוֹם) – Peace; wholeness, flourishing, harmony.
- Tamim (תָּמִים) – Blameless, whole, mature.
- Lev (לֵב) – Heart; the center of thought and devotion.
- Qahal (קָהָל) – Assembly; God's gathered people.
- Shem (שֵׁם) – Name; identity, reputation, character.
- Nahal (נָחַל) – To inherit; passing on legacy.

Greek Terms

- Basileia (βασιλεία) – Kingdom, reign, rule.
- Ekklesia (ἐκκλησία) – Church, called-out assembly.
- Laos (λαός) – People of God.
- Exousia (ἐξουσία) – Authority, delegated power.
- Dynamis (δύναμις) – Power, supernatural ability.
- Kratos (κράτος) – Strength, dominion.
- Teleios (τέλειος) – Mature, complete.
- Hodos (ὁδός) – Way, path of discipleship.
- Parousia (παρουσία) – Coming, presence of Christ.
- Eschatos (ἔσχατος) – Last, final; root of eschatology.

- Apokatastasis (ἀποκατάστασις) – Restoration, renewal.
- Dipsychos (δίψυχος) – Double-minded, unstable.
- Homologeō (ὁμολογέω) – Confess, agree with God.
- Diakonia (διακονία) – Service, ministry.
- Martyria (μαρτυρία) – Witness, testimony.

Appendix D

Study and Reflection Questions

- Use these questions for personal meditation, small groups, or leadership training.

Kingdom Mindset Renewal

- Where are you most tempted to conform to culture rather than Kingdom truth?
- What disciplines help you renew your mind daily?

Watchmen, Priests, and Gatekeepers

- What role of spiritual guardianship do you carry in your family or community?

Holiness and Distinction

- What compromises must you resist to remain set apart?

Covenant Faithfulness

- How can you ensure that the next generation inherits Kingdom truth?

Kingdom Culture

- How do you engage culture without assimilation?

Ethics and Justice

- Where can you embody God's justice today in tangible ways?

Legacy and Succession

- Who are you intentionally preparing to carry forward Kingdom influence?

All Things New

- How does the eternal horizon shape your daily priorities?

Authority and Leadership

- How do you walk under authority so you can lead rightly?

The Eternal Journey

- Where do you need to keep pressing toward maturity instead of settling?

The King's People, The King's Reign

- How does your unity with other believers reveal the reign of Christ?

Appendix E

Kingdom Practices for Daily Life

Kingdom life requires daily practices that sustain faith and form maturity. These practices are not burdens but gifts, shaping us to live under the reign of Christ.

Learning and Study – Immerse yourself in Scripture, for the Word is the King's wisdom given to His people. To study is to submit to formation.

> *"Your word is a lamp to my feet and a light to my path."*
>
> *Psalm 119:105*

Worship and Participation – Worship is surrender, not performance. Corporate participation is essential; it unites us as one voice before the throne.

> *"Come, let us worship and bow down; let us kneel before the Lord, our Maker."*
>
> *Psalm 95:6*

Prayer and Intercession – Continual dialogue with God aligns our hearts and releases His will into the earth.

> *"Pray without ceasing."*
>
> *1 Thessalonians 5:17*

Fasting and Discipline – Denying the flesh clarifies devotion and strengthens spiritual authority.

Fellowship and Community – Life together forms accountability and encouragement. The Kingdom is not lived in isolation.

> *"And they devoted themselves to the apostles' teaching and the fellowship, to the breaking of bread and the prayers."*
>
> *Acts 2:42*

Acts of Justice and Mercy – Daily fairness, compassion, and advocacy reveal the King's heart in society.

> *"He has shown you, O man, what is good… to do justice, to love mercy, and to walk humbly with your God."*
>
> *Micah 6:8*

Stewardship and Generosity – All resources belong to the King. We are stewards, not owners, called to generosity and wise management.

> *"The earth is the Lord's and the fullness thereof."*
>
> *Psalm 24:1*

Sabbath and Rest – Rest resists the idolatry of busyness and teaches dependence on God.

Witness and Mission – Every believer is an ambassador. Our lives testify daily to the reign of Christ.

"You will be my witnesses… to the end of the earth."

Acts 1:8

Closing Word

These appendices are not add-ons but pathways. They guide Kingdom citizens into formation, alignment, study, worship, and mission. They invite us to embody the truths of Kingdomish not as theory but as daily life. Through them, the Spirit trains us for maturity, prepares us for eternity, and enables us to live now in the fullness of the King's reign.

READER'S CHARGE

A Covenant of Kingdom Citizenship

Having read and embraced the message of Kingdomish, I recognize that the call of the King is not only to believe but to embody. I confess that my life is not my own, for I have been bought with a price. I belong to the King, and I pledge myself to live as His citizen in this world until He comes in glory.

I will renew my mind daily, rejecting conformity to this age and embracing the transformation of the Spirit.

I will pursue holiness and justice, for righteousness and justice are the foundation of His throne.

I will walk in covenant faithfulness, preparing the next generation to carry forward what has been entrusted to me.

I will guard the unity of the King's people, resisting division, and embodying love.

I will walk under authority so that I may exercise authority rightly, serving rather than dominating.

I will embrace the eternal journey, pressing on toward maturity, not settling in complacency.

I will set my eyes on the eternal horizon, living now in light of the Consummation when all things will be made new.

I will study diligently, worship wholeheartedly, pray persistently, act justly, give generously, and live missionally.

I make this charge before God and His people, not in my strength but in His grace.

I will live Kingdomish—anchored in the reign of Christ, aligned with His Word, and empowered by His Spirit—until the day the King Himself appears and declares:

"Well done, good and faithful servant. Enter into the joy of your Lord."

Matthew 25:21

Signature: _____ Date: _____

ABOUT THE AUTHORS

Kim Parks

Founder and Chair of Master Builders Kingdom Leadership Academy (MBKLA), Parks is the visionary force behind OmniVertex Group and OmniVertex Press. With a mandate to raise Kingdom leaders across generations, she has dedicated her life to teaching, writing, and equipping believers to embody the culture and authority of God's Kingdom in every sphere of life.

Through MBKLA, Parks develops leaders through discipleship, formation, and rigorous academic training rooted in Scripture. She is committed to bridging spiritual formation and practical leadership, preparing leaders to walk in holiness, justice, and covenant faithfulness.

As lead author of the Kingdom Formation Series, Parks calls readers beyond cultural Christianity into transformational Kingdom citizenship. Her works weave together theology, biblical studies, and practical application to inspire a generation to live "All Kingdom, All the Time."

Ezra Pryor

Vice Chair and Co-Founder of MBKLA, Pryor serves as co-author of Kingdomish, contributing expertise in finance, compliance, and strategic development. He has been instrumental in shaping MBKLA's organizational framework and ensuring that its Kingdom mandate is carried out with integrity and sustainability.

With a background in finance and operational leadership, Pryor brings practical insight to the theological vision of the series. His contribution to Kingdomish highlights the importance of sound structure, wise stewardship, and faithful leadership in advancing the Kingdom across generations.

Together, Parks and Pryor embody the collaborative spirit of Kingdom leadership. Their shared work in MBKLA and the Kingdom Formation Series reflects a unified commitment: to raise up a people who embody the character of the King, steward His influence with integrity, and prepare for the consummation of His reign.

You were never called to live Kingdom-ish.

Too many believers settle for partial obedience, inherited religion, and cultural compromise. Kingdom-ish exposes the barriers, boundaries, and beliefs that keep us from fully integrating Kingdom life.

Through biblical insights, Hebrew and Greek word studies, and practical spiritual formation, this foundational work equips you to:

- ✔ Renew your mindset.
- ✔ Realign your identity.

✔ Break free from internal resistance.

✔ Fully embody Kingdom living.

Kingdom-ish is more than a book—it is a call to transformation, preparing you for the journey ahead in the Kingdom Formation Series.

NOTES / INDEX